Getting a Grip on the Basics of Prosperous Living

by
Beth Jones

VALLEY PRESS
PUBLISHERS
Portage, MI

2nd Printing

Getting a Grip on the Basics of Prosperous Living
ISBN 1-57794-009-1
Copyright © 1997 by Beth Jones
P. O. Box 555
Richland, Michigan 49083

Published by Valley Press Publishers
995 Romence Road
Portage, MI 49024

Contents

Acknowledgments

I am deeply indebted to many people whom the Lord has used to teach and to enlighten me on this subject of prosperous living.

First and foremost, I would not know or be able to write anything were it not for the grace of God. I appreciate God's grace, the blood of Jesus and the ministry of the Holy Spirit in my own life and ministry. I know that apart from Him I can do nothing.

Second, I am blessed to have a loving and supportive husband, Jeff, who has consistently encouraged me to do all God has put in my heart. I am thankful to have wonderful parents, Jerry Shepard and Carol Barker, who instilled within me as a child a "nothing is impossible" attitude.

Third, I want to acknowledge those who have prayed for me and for this project. I especially want to thank seven people who agreed to be prayer partners with me at a time when I needed their undergirding and during the writing of this book:

Cindy Boester

Michelle Clowe

Kate Cook

Tara Copps

Cathy Creek

Mary Jo Fox

Andrea Hammack

Introduction

You have incredible potential! It is my prayer that, as you study through this workbook and look up the Scriptures in your own Bible, you will become absolutely convinced that God wants to prosper your life!

I trust that you will see the two main reasons He wants you to prosper: first, because He loves you and wants you to be blessed abundantly; and second, because He loves others and wants to use you to be a blessing to humanity for the Gospel's sake. I am thoroughly convinced that God wants you to be blessed and to be a blessing to others! I believe God Himself will convince you of these truths as you study His Word on this subject.

As enthusiastic as I am about the subject of prosperity, I realize that, when you mention prosperity and success, people will have a variety of responses because of their various experiences and backgrounds. Every person looks at this subject through different-colored glasses, so this workbook was written with many types of people in mind.

- Perhaps you're a believer who has never studied the subject of prosperous living. Maybe your only experience with this subject has been the lack of prosperity and the never-ending cycle of struggling to make ends meet. This study in God's Word will set you free!

- Perhaps the thought of prosperity brings a sense of great excitement, a thought that it's almost too good to be true. As you study God's Word your heart will be filled with faith for God's blessings.

- Perhaps the thought that God would prosper people almost sounds like heresy to you. Sure, you believe in spiritual prosperity, but the thought of God prospering His people financially and materially seems almost like a worldly concept. Allow this workbook to help you rightly divide God's Word on this important subject.

- Perhaps the subject of prosperity brings you condemnation and reminds you of a "prosperity venture" that crashed and burned, and you still haven't been able to figure out why. As you study God's Word your questions will be answered and your faith will be rebuilt.

- Perhaps you're one of the naive ones who thinks the "prosperity message" is another term for "lazy faith" — the kind of faith that causes a person to lean back in his recliner, just waiting for the mailman to fill the mailbox with all those prosperity checks! This workbook will help you to get the big picture and an understanding of how the natural and supernatural work together.

- Perhaps you're one of those sincere Christians who knows that God desires for you to experience prosperity. You have tithed and have given offerings and alms, but you haven't really seen the harvest of prosperity in your life. Maybe you see prosperity as a great theory but have not yet experienced its reality. As you study God's Word you will receive the revelation you need to experience prosperity!

- Perhaps you're a high school or college student with your whole life out there in front of you. You need to realize that God has a good plan for your life. If you will do things God's way,

He will teach you to profit and show you the way you should go! Put the principles of God's Word into practice and God will do exceedingly, abundantly above all you could ask or think!

- Perhaps you're in the middle of your career or vocation, or maybe in your latter years, and you think it's too late for God to really prosper you like He could if you were young enough to start over. But God is the God of the impossible, isn't He? If you will make the necessary adjustments in your thinking, in your believing and, where necessary, in your behavior, God can do more for you in one day than you could have done in a thousand years of work. It's *never* too late with God and this study in God's Word will be an encouragement to you!

This workbook will be good news for each and every type of person just described. As the Lord tells us in Hosea 4:6, **My people are destroyed for lack of knowledge.** The purpose of this workbook is to help you obtain the knowledge of God's Word on the important subject of prosperous living. You will study it for yourself from the Word of God — from Genesis to Revelation. As you study these Scriptures, the Holy Spirit, Who is your Teacher, will guide you into all truth; and when you know the truth, it will set you free! (John 14:16,17,26; 8:31,32.)

So, you are about to enter into the study of an exciting subject! Because it's so exciting, the devil has worked for years to hoodwink sincere Christians in this area. Believers have thought that poverty and lack were "God's will for them." They have thought that it was "worldly or carnal to be wealthy." Many Christians have been deceived by the world's double standard thinking! As believers, we have agreed that it is perfectly acceptable for a CEO, a professional athlete, an entrepreneur, a movie star, or a sweepstakes or lottery winner to be wealthy and prosperous. In fact, oftentimes, we applaud their riches as well-deserved! But for some reason, as soon as a hard working Christian or a worker in the church, or God forbid — a pastor, traveling evangelist, teacher, missionary, or other preacher begins to prosper in a substantial way, people (including some well-meaning Christians) begin to question their motives and credibility. Why this double standard? If anyone ought to be blessed — it ought to be the child of God! (If you think about it many pastors and ministers in addition to their expertise and anointing to minister are also required to function as CEO's of large organizations!) Shouldn't we applaud and rejoice when a member of God's family, a person who worships and serves Jesus Christ, prospers in a significant way? Why should the person who rejects Jesus Christ and even openly pledges allegiance to Satan be admired for their prosperity? This doesn't make any rational sense! The result of this kind of thinking has caused financial frustration among believers and a lack of abundant funds for financing the Gospel around the world. Frustrating Christians and hindering the Gospel — don't those sound like things the devil would be behind? It's time for Christians to quit apologizing for God's blessings! It's time Christians quit feeling as though they have to defend their right to be prosperous!

The purpose of this book is to help Christians study the Word of God in detail so that prosperity becomes a way of life for multitudes in the body of Christ. In our own personal experience, my husband and I have known both the despair of lack and the joy of prosperity. We are probably like many of you. As a family, we have known the difficulty of making ends meet. We have felt the weight of being in debt up to our eyeballs and have experienced the hardship of making bad financial decisions. We know what it's like to start at the bottom. We have lived in the tiny, "handyman special" homes and we have driven those "economy cars!" But over the years, we have gotten hold of the truth of God's Word in this area of prosperous living from both the spiritual side and the natural side.

As we have stayed consistent in our believing and in our giving, it has been exciting to watch God's Word work for us! God has given us wisdom in the financial affairs of our lives. He has opened doors and given us the knowledge of prosperous, witty, innovative ideas when needed. And we have endeavored to be good stewards over the gifts and talents He has entrusted us with. The result is that we have experienced the Lord's abundant blessings both financially and materially. Prosperous living is no longer just a theory — it's a reality that continues to increase each year. This is our desire for you as well!

I promise you, the light of God's Word will make a profound change in your life. Again, I want to say, you are a person of incredible potential! In this area of prosperous living, it is our prayer that you will receive confidence in God's will for your prosperity. Not only that, it is our desire that you receive enlightenment in both the natural and spiritual areas so that you may experience prosperous living for yourself! Remember, prosperous living comes for two reasons: God loves you and wants you to be blessed abundantly; and second, God loves others and He wants to use you to be a blessing to humanity for the Gospel's sake!

As you study the Scriptures, may you become personally convinced of God's willingness to do exceedingly and abundantly above and beyond all that you could hope or ask for in this area of your life. (Eph. 3:20.) God bless you as you study His Word.

GUIDELINES FOR STUDY

A. GUIDELINES FOR INDIVIDUAL STUDY

1. Set aside a regular time each week when you can get alone with God and study the lessons in this workbook.

2. Pray and ask the Lord to illuminate His Word to you each time you study.

3. Look up each Scripture and take time to think upon the Word of God.

4. Don't be in a hurry to complete the workbook; rather, move through the book at a steady pace and allow the Holy Spirit to minister to you personally.

B. GUIDELINES FOR GROUP STUDY

1. A group can consist of two or more people. It is important to have one leader, preferably a mature Christian, who can facilitate the group study and discussion.

2. Determine a regular time and a quiet location for the group to meet together to study the lessons in this workbook each week.

3. Pray and ask the Lord to illuminate His Word each week.

4. Look up the Scriptures and take turns reading them aloud.

5. Make each person in the group feel welcome and important; encourage each one to participate. Don't allow one person to dominate all the discussion.

6. Take time to allow for group discussion and interaction during the lessons, but avoid getting off track with side issues.

7. Don't be in a hurry to complete the workbook; rather, maintain a steady progression through the lessons and allow the Holy Spirit the freedom to minister to each individual in the group.

8. It is wise to assign the next lesson as homework each week. After the group members have done their individual study, they will be more familiar with the material. Encourage group members to write down any questions they might have and present them for discussion the next time you meet together.

FIRST THINGS FIRST

Before you begin this study in prosperous living, we want to put first things first. Prosperity begins when you enter into a personal relationship with Jesus Christ. Your spiritual prosperity is of foremost importance, and for that reason we want to take a moment to share God's plan for your spiritual prosperity.

God's original plan for you was that you would enjoy a personal relationship with Him. However, as you know, mankind chose to sin; they disobeyed God's voice, and the relationship between God and man was severed. Because of God's great love for man, He sent His Son, Jesus Christ, to cleanse us from sin and to pay the penalty that sin demanded. Perhaps these Scriptures are familiar to you:

> **For God so loved the world, that he gave his only begotten Son, that whosoever believeth in him should not perish, but have everlasting life.**
>
> **John 3:16**

> **For all have sinned, and come short of the glory of God.**
>
> **Romans 3:23**

> **For the wages of sin is death; but the gift of God is eternal life through Jesus Christ our Lord.**
>
> **Romans 6:23**

When Jesus died on the cross, He paid the wages of sin in His death; and when He rose from the dead, He offered mankind the opportunity to be righteous (without sin) in God's sight once again. Jesus Christ died on the cross so our sins could be forgiven and we could enjoy a personal relationship with God once again. Each one of us has to make a choice: either believe in and receive Jesus Christ as our Lord, or reject Him. God will never twist your arm; the choice is up to you. He loves you, and He sent His Son to die for you, but you still have the right to exercise your free will to accept or reject Jesus Christ as your Lord.

> **Jesus saith unto him, I am the way, the truth, and the life: no man cometh unto the Father, but by me.**
>
> **John 14:6**

> **That if thou shalt confess with thy mouth the Lord Jesus, and shalt believe in thine heart that God hath raised him from the dead, thou shalt be saved.**
>
> **Romans 10:9**

If you have never received Jesus Christ by confessing Him as your Lord, then pray a prayer like this from your heart:

> Dear God, I come to You in the name of Jesus. I need You. I know that I'm a sinner in need of a Savior. Jesus, I believe that You died for me and were raised from the dead by God. I believe that You are the Lord, so I now confess You as my Lord. Thank You that I am now saved and a part of Your family.

If you have prayed this prayer for the first time, we would suggest that you obtain the workbook entitled, *Getting a Grip on the Basics*. It will help you to grow in your relationship with Jesus Christ.

CHAPTER ONE

"WHAT IS PROSPEROUS LIVING?"
PROSPERITY DEFINED

What is your definition of prosperity? As we begin our study of prosperous living, we want to take a few moments to define our terms. Are we just talking about spiritual prosperity? Are we talking about material prosperity, financial prosperity, and physical prosperity? Are we talking about prosperity in other areas of our lives, such as our families, our relationships, or our service to God? What is prosperity?

We understand that because of religious traditions, past experiences and stereotypical thinking, people have defined prosperity in a variety of ways. There are those who, through greed and covetousness, have taken the "prosperity message" into a ditch and have given the true biblical definition of prosperity a black eye. There are those on the other side of the ditch who define true prosperity as a lifestyle of poverty even a "vow of poverty." To them, this is somehow more noble and pleasing to God.

There are various other ideas and definitions of prosperity. Some people define prosperity as God's willingness to meet our "needs" but not our "wants." Others believe He only chooses to bless those He can trust with prosperity. (What does this say about the person who isn't prospering — that God can't trust him or her?) Still others define prosperous living in terms of their spiritual prosperity; they are convinced that God just isn't in the business of prospering people financially or materially.

We can see then that there are many views and definitions concerning prosperity. Our goal in this study is to find out how God defines prosperity.

Prosperity is a broad subject. As we study the subject of prosperous living, we will find that God's blessing of prosperity in our lives affects our spiritual and physical lives, our relationships, our vocation, and our effectiveness in ministry, as well as our material and financial condition. However, the focal point of our study in this workbook will be to discover what the Bible teaches us about financial and material prosperity. We will be looking specifically at what God has to say about a Christian's relationship to money, riches and wealth.

We must approach this subject of prosperous living with an open mind, trusting that the Holy Spirit will guide us into all the truth. (With all due respect, we aren't interested in what you think, in what some preacher says, in what your mother or father told you or in what your friend has experienced.) We are interested in finding out what the Bible says concerning God's will on prosperous living. To do so, we will use several chapters in this study to lay a scriptural foundation.

Let's begin our study by looking at God's will for our prosperity. (This chapter will include several definitions and some technical words. We've tried to make it simple as we lay a scriptural foundation.)

A. GOD'S WILL FOR OUR PROSPERITY

Is prosperity God's will for His people? Is prosperous living the desire of God's heart for His children? Or is the "prosperity message" just a carnal, fleshly doctrine propagated by those who are "lovers of money"?

What has God told us about His will for the prosperity of His people in these Scriptures?

1. Psalm 35:27

   What gives the Lord pleasure? _____

   Who does God want to prosper?_____

   Are you a servant of God? _____

   According to this verse, would it please God to see you prosper? _____
   _____

   What does the first part of this verse tell you to do?_____
   _____

   Take a moment to picture God delighting in your prosperity. Have you ever imagined that your prosperity blesses Him? _____

   From a parental point of view, why do you think God wants His children to prosper? __
   _____

   PROSPERITY: The Hebrew word for "prosperity" is *shalowm* or *shalom* (pronounced *shaw-lome'*).[1] Its meaning includes safety, welfare, health, prosperity, peace and rest. We can see that God's definition of prosperity is all-encompassing!

2. Proverbs 10:22

   What does the blessing of the Lord do in your life? _____
   _____

   What do you think "maketh rich" means? _____
   _____

What does "he addeth no sorrow with it" mean? _____
_____

In your own words, how would you describe being rich "with no sorrow"?_____
_____

Did you know it is possible to become rich without the Lord's blessing? That's true, but it comes with sorrow. People can work hard, enslaving themselves to their jobs or businesses, and become rich. However, in the process they can lose their marriage, their kids, their health, their peace of mind, their joy of living, and can even die prematurely. When we do things God's way, He makes us rich and adds no sorrow with it!

RICH: The Hebrew word for "rich" is *ashar* (pronounced *aw-shar'*).[2] Its meaning includes to accumulate, to make self rich, to grow rich.

3. Ecclesiastes 5:19

    What did Solomon describe as the "gift of God"? _____
    _____
    _____

4. Isaiah 48:17

    What two things did your Redeemer say He would do for you? _____
    _____
    _____

    Do you think God would ever teach you something or lead you in a way that was contrary to His will? _____
    _____

    If He is going to teach you to profit and lead you in the way you should go, can you conclude that it is His will for you to profit? _____

    PROFIT: The Hebrew word for "profit" is *ya'al* (pronounced *yaw-al'*).[3] Its meaning includes to ascend, to benefit and to be valuable.

5. John 10:10

    What did Jesus say He came to bring?_____

    How would you define *abundant life*?_____

    If you were in poverty and lack, would that be abundant life? _____

Let's see what the Greek words for "life" and "abundantly" mean.

LIFE: The Greek word for "life" is *zoe* (pronounced *dzo-ay'*).[4] Its meaning includes the absolute fullness of life. The God-kind of life which He imparts to man!

ABUNDANTLY: The Greek word for "abundantly" is *perissos* (pronounced *per-is-sos'*).[5] Its meaning includes more than is necessary, superadded, extraordinary, surpassing, the sense of beyond, superabundant in quantity or superior in quality, excessive, preeminence, exceedingly abundantly above, more abundantly, beyond measure.

Do you get the idea from these definitions that God's will for His children includes something above and beyond average? _____

6. Romans 8:32

    What was the most precious gift God ever gave to mankind? _____
    _____

    What else does God say He will give us? _____
    _____

    What could "all things" include? _____
    _____

7. Ephesians 3:20

    What does God want to do?_____
    _____

    Do you see God's will for your prosperity in this verse?_____

8. 3 John 2

    What did the Holy Spirit, through the apostle John, tell us God desired above all things?
    _____
    _____
    _____

    What type of prosperity was He describing? _____
    _____

    Our prosperity and our health are supposed to be in proportion to what? _____
    _____

    Is your soul prospering? _____

PROSPER: The Greek word for "prosper" is *euodoo* (pronounced *yoo-od-o'-o*).[6] Its meaning includes to succeed in reaching, to succeed in business affairs, a prosperous journey, to cause to prosper and be successful.

It is clear from these initial Scriptures that God desires His people to prosper!

Let's take a moment to look at the opposite side of prosperity; that is, poverty and lack. We can learn much about what something is by looking at what it is not. Let's see what the Bible has to say about poverty and lack — what it is, who it is for and where it comes from. In particular, we want to answer this question: Is God the Author of poverty and lack for His divine reasons?

9. Psalm 34:10

    Will those who seek the Lord have lack?_____

10. Proverbs 6:6-11; 20:13

    What is the cause of poverty in these passages? _____
    _____

    What can we learn from the ant? _____
    _____

11. Proverbs 10:15

    What destroys the poor? _____

    Is God in the business of destroying people for His divine purpose? _____
    _____

12. Proverbs 11:24

    What is the cause of poverty in this Scripture?_____
    _____

    What resulted for the giving person?_____
    _____

13. Proverbs 13:18

    According to this verse, what causes poverty?_____
    _____

14. Proverbs 23:21

   What three things will cause a person to be in poverty?

   _____   _____   _____

15. Proverbs 24:30-34

   What was the cause of poverty in this passage?_____
   _____

   In your own words, describe the missing elements in this person's work ethic. _____
   _____
   _____

16. Proverbs 28:19

   What type of person shall have plenty?_____

   What type of person shall have poverty? _____

17. Proverbs 28:27

   Who shall not suffer lack? _____

It is evident from these passages on poverty and lack that God is not the Author of either one of them! In fact, it's quite clear that a person who lacks discipline, wisdom and a strong work ethic will bring poverty upon himself or herself. God expects us to work diligently, and we will study this aspect of prosperous living in another chapter.

Now that we know God wants us to prosper, we must determine from the Bible God's definition of prosperity.

B. GOD'S DEFINITION OF OUR PROSPERITY

We will find that God uses a variety of terms and examples to define prosperity. Although our main focus during the course of this book is on God's plan for our prosperity in the material and financial areas, in this section we want to take a brief look at four basic areas of prosperity: spiritual blessings, material blessings, financial blessings and relational blessings. (Prosperity also includes the physical blessings of our health and healing; however, we won't be studying the subject of healing in this workbook.)[7]

Once we've looked at these four basic areas of prosperity, we will study several words that help us to biblically define prosperity. It is important that we understand the vocabulary words God uses when He defines and reveals His will concerning our prosperity. If you have ever studied a foreign language or a specific subject in school or in a university, you may recall that some of the first things you learned were the vocabulary words for that particular subject and their definitions.

We see that God describes and defines prosperity in many ways. Sometimes He uses words that are obvious: prosperity, prosper, profit, riches and wealth. At other times He uses words and phrases that imply prosperity, such as abundance, increase, fruitful, multiply, substance and treasures. I like these words; they paint such a generous picture of God! We will see that God isn't talking about "just making ends meet," but about an incredible, overflowing, excess, surplus type of prosperity.

1. Four basic areas of prosperity:

    Look up the following verses and determine which type of prosperity God was giving to His people. Place a check mark in all the appropriate columns which define the type of prosperity we see in each of these Scriptures:

SCRIPTURE	SPIRITUAL	MATERIAL	FINANCIAL	RELATIONAL
Genesis 13:6				
Genesis 24:21				
Genesis 24:40				
Genesis 24:42				
Deuteronomy 8:13				
Deuteronomy 11:6-18				
Deuteronomy 28:2-14				
Deuteronomy 29:9				
Joshua 1:7, 8				
1 Kings 2:3				
Nehemiah 1:11				

SCRIPTURE	SPIRITUAL	MATERIAL	FINANCIAL	RELATIONAL
Nehemiah 2:20				
Psalm 1:3				
Psalm 112:1-3				
Proverbs 8:21				
Proverbs 15:6				
Proverbs 24:3,4				
Romans 1:10				
Romans 10:12				
2 Corinthians 6:10				
2 Timothy 3:16				

2. Abundance:

God is not the God of "just get by." Did you know that? He called Himself the Almighty God. In the Hebrew, that literally means *El Shaddai* — the God Who is more than enough! (Gen. 17:1.) God is not, as some have coined the phrase, "El Cheapo — the God of just get by." He's the God of abundance! The very words *abundant, abundance,* and *abundantly* imply something that is overflowing, in excess and more than enough! Let's look again, in a little more detail at the Hebrew and Greek definitions for these words.

ABUNDANTLY: We are going to look at three Hebrew words translated as "abundantly." One of the Hebrew words for "abundantly" is *sharats* (pronounced *shraw-rats'*).[8] Its meaning includes to swarm or abound.

Another Hebrew word is *rob* (pronounced *robe*).[9] Its meaning includes great number, huge, be increased, more or number, much, multitude, plenty.

A third Hebrew word is *rabah* (pronounced *raw-baw*).[10] Its meaning includes to increase in whatever respect, enlarge, excel, heap, plenty, and multiply.

As we have already seen, the Greek word for "abundantly" is *perissos* (pronounced *per-is-sos'*).[11] It can be summarized by its meaning of superabundant in quantity or superior in quality, excessive and beyond measure.

a. Genesis 1:20,21; 8:17; 9:7

What type of picture do you get from these passages about man and God's creation? What words can you use to describe this?_____

_____

b. 2 Samuel 12:30

David won a battle and brought forth what? _____

_____

c. 1 Chronicles 22:3,4,14,15; 29:2

Describe David's preparations for the house of the Lord. _____

_____

Do you get the idea that David was on a tight budget? _____

d. 2 Chronicles 1:7-15

God abundantly blessed Solomon. We see evidence of this in verses 13-15.

How many chariots did he have? _____

How many horsemen did he have? _____

How plenteous was the silver and gold?_____

e. 1 Kings 10:1-24

In verses 4-8, the queen of Sheba was able to witness firsthand the prosperity of King Solomon. What evidence did she see that God had blessed Solomon with wisdom, riches, wealth and honor?_____

_____

_____

According to verses 2 and 10, what type of gifts did the queen of Sheba give to God's servant, Solomon, and in what quantity? _____

_____

_____

A TALENT OF GOLD: Authorities differ on the exact modern equivalent of a "talent" of gold. *Smith's Bible Dictionary, The Thompson Chain Reference Bible* and *Dake's Annotated Reference Bible* all use the figure of $29,085 American dollars as the modern equivalent of 1 "talent" of gold.[12] To stay on the conservative side we will use these figures as well, plus we will calculate the modern day equivalent using these figures.

Authorities agree that 1 "talent" of gold is roughly equivalent to 125 Troy pounds. Additionally, there are 12 Troy ounces per Troy pound, or 1500 Troy ounces in each "talent" of gold.

Therefore, if 1 talent of gold equals 125 Troy pounds or 1500 Troy ounces, and the current price of gold is at $350 per Troy ounce, then 1 "talent" of gold would be equivalent to $525,000 in our modern day equivalent. We will give both the conservative and the modern day equivalents in our calculations.

THE QUEEN OF SHEBA'S GIFT:

Using these two different calculations, we find that the 120 talents of gold the queen of Sheba gave to Solomon were equal to $3,490,200 on the conservative side, and $63,000,000 using the current price of gold. In either case, her gift was substantial!

Was the queen of Sheba an abundant giver? _____

In verses 10-23, we see a description of Solomon's riches and wealth. What types of things are itemized?_____

_____

_____

How would you describe the quantity and quality of the riches and wealth God had caused Solomon to have?

Quantity: _____

Quality: _____

The next time you wonder if God wants you to have abundance, just remember King Solomon. God demonstrated what His definition of riches and wealth were in the way He blessed Solomon! For further inspiration, look up Matthew 6:25-34; consider God's reference to Solomon and his glory — which was given to him of the Lord — and meditate upon God's promise to bless you as you seek first His kingdom. This passage should shed new light on what God means when He says He will add all these things to you!

f.   2 Chronicles 17:5; 18:1,2; 20:25

How would you describe the life of God's servant, Jehoshaphat? _____

_____

According to chapter 17, verse 5, and chapter 18, verse 1, what did he have in abundance? _____

g. John 10:10

What did Jesus come to bring to believers?_____

_____

h. Ephesians 3:20

How does God want to bless His people? _____

_____

3. Increase:

Here we see another word that implies prosperity.

INCREASE: We are looking at three Hebrew words for "increase." One is *yacaph* (pronounced *yaw-saf*).[13] It means to add, to increase and to do again, continue, exceed, get more. The second is *tebuwah* (pronounced *teb-oo-aw*).[14] It means income, produce, gain, and revenue. The third is *rabah* (pronounced *raw-baw*).[15] It means abundance, full of, enlarge, heap, multiply, and plenty.

a. Psalm 115:14

What will the Lord do for us and our children?_____

_____

b. Proverbs 3:9

What are we to honor the Lord with? _____

_____

Increase by definition implies that we would not decrease! To honor the Lord with the first fruits of our increase tells us that we should be increasing, gaining and being added unto!

c. Proverbs 13:11

Wealth gotten by vanity does what? _____

Wealth gotten by labor does what? _____

d. 1 Corinthians 3:6,7

Oftentimes in the Bible, we see the word *increase* being used as an agricultural term. We see it used in both the Old and New Testaments in reference to sowing, reaping and increasing. In this passage, we see a principle of increase. Although this particular passage is talking about sowing the spiritual seed of God's Word into the lives of believers, we can glean some things that are important to know concerning God's laws of increase.

Who sows and waters the seed? _____

What does God give? _____

Could God give the increase if we didn't do our part to sow and water the seed? ____
_____
_____

This is a good Bible principle to be aware of. We will study the subject of sowing and reaping in more detail in a later chapter, but we wanted to introduce it here.

4. Fruitful:

God wants us to be fruitful in all the areas of our lives, and this is no less true in the material and financial areas.

a. Genesis 1:22,28; 8:17; 9:1,7; 17:6,20; 28:3; 35:11; 48:4

According to the Book of Beginnings, Genesis, we clearly see that God's will for His people was what?_____
_____

To be fruitful is certainly a reference to the reproduction of man after his kind, as well as animals and seed-bearing trees after their kind. To produce children is truly one of God's great blessings to mankind, but the word *fruitful* means more than that. In Hebrew, to be fruitful means more than just reproduction. This word implies something that is the result of a seed. Certainly, that relates to reproduction, but in later chapters we will see that we can sow various types of seed and expect them to be fruitful!

FRUITFUL: The Hebrew word for "fruitful" is *parah* (pronounced *paw-raw'*).[16] It means to bear fruit, be fruitful, to make fruitful, grow and increase.

b. Colossians 1:10

What does God want believers to do? _____

5. Multiply:

Again, we see the words *fruitful* and *multiply* coupled in many passages of Scripture, but we will find that God's idea of multiplying us includes more than bearing generations of children.

MULTIPLY: The Hebrew word for "multiply" is *rabah* (pronounced *raw-baw'*).[17] The same word is translated as abundance and increase. Its meaning includes to increase in whatever respect, bring in abundance, enlarge, exceedingly, be full of, heap, multiply, plenty.

a. Genesis 1:22,28; 8:17; 9:1; 17:2,20; 22:17; 26:4,24; 28:3; 35:11; 48:4

Again, from the Book of Beginnings, what is God's will for His people? _____
_____

It is clear that God is talking about multitudes of Israelites being born generation after generation. The picture is made clear when God told Abraham to look at the stars of the sky and the sand of the seashore. This is God's idea of multiplying!

In addition to multiplying children, what else does God want to multiply in our lives?

b. Deuteronomy 7:13

Now that you have a picture of what God means when He says to multiply, what did God expand His multiple blessings to include? _____
_____

c. Deuteronomy 8:13

What five specific areas did the Lord say would be multiplied?

_____   _____

_____   _____

_____

Would God's definition of "multiply" for "herds and flocks" be any different than His definition of "multiply" for "silver, gold and all that you have"? _____

In your own words, describe what your life would be like if God were to multiply your "silver, gold and all that you have". _____

d. 2 Corinthians 9:10

Based upon what we know God's definition of "multiply" to be, what does God say will happen to the seed you sow? _____

When studying this passage later in the book, we will find that the seed being referred to in this passage is literally financial seed!

6. Substance:

This is a good word! Substance is talking about material things.

SUBSTANCE: There are three Hebrew words we want to look at: One is *rekuwsh* (pronounced *rek-oosh'*) or *rekush* (pronounced *rekoosh'*), which means property, goods, riches, substance.[18] The other is *yesh* (pronounced *yaysh*), which means being, existence, substance.[19] The third is *hown* (pronounced *hone*) which means wealth, enough, riches, substance.[20]

a. Genesis 12:5; 13:6

How do these verses describe the prosperity of God's servant, Abram (Abraham); his wife, Sarai (Sarah); and his nephew, Lot? _____
_____

Can you see that they had a lot of "stuff?" _____

When was the last time you had to move to another city because the town you lived in couldn't hold all your "stuff?"_____

Abraham, God's covenant man, was a person of massive wealth! We will study his life in more detail in another chapter.

b. 2 Chronicles 32:27-30

Hezekiah, another of God's servants, was also quite rich. How do these verses describe God's blessing in his life? _____
_____

Who gave him his "substance?" _____

c. Job 1:3

There may be some things we don't understand about Job; but from this verse, what one thing is clear about this man of God?_____
_____

d. Proverbs 8:21

If we love the wisdom of God, what does He cause us to inherit? _____
_____

e. Proverbs 28:8

What is the wrong way to gain "substance?" _____

_____

f. Proverbs 3:9

What are we to do with our "substance?" _____

_____

What type of "substance" do you have? _____

_____

Are you giving God the first fruits of your "substance?" _____

g. Luke 8:3

What did these believing women, Joanna, Susanna and many others, minister to (or honor) Jesus with? _____

_____

What do you think this was a reference to? _____

_____

h. Luke 15:13

The prodigal son is an example of someone who did not honor the Lord with his substance.

From this passage, what can we determine that his substance consisted of? _____

_____

What did he do with his substance? _____

_____

Can you see that God wants us to be blessed with "substance" — things that will be a blessing to us and with which we can honor Him?

7. Treasures:

TREASURES: The Hebrew word for "treasures" is *owtsar* (pronounced *o-tsaw'*).[21] It means treasure, storehouse, treasure house, and depository.

a. Proverbs 8:21

If we seek wisdom, what will happen to our treasures?_____

_____

b. Proverbs 15:6

What is in the house of the righteous? _____

c. Proverbs 21:20

What is in the dwelling of the wise?_____

Treasures are the by-product of God's wisdom and His blessing in our lives.

We can see that God's will is for His people to be prosperous, and God's definition of prosperity is superabundance! There is nothing in God's definition that resembles lack or poverty or "just barely getting along." We have seen that God uses a variety of words and phrases to convey the idea of prosperity, each of them implying excess, overflow, above and beyond what we can ask or think! Are you beginning to get the idea that God wants you to prosper in life?

Now a word of caution and encouragement:

These Scriptures and these concepts may be new to some of you, and you may have several questions. We will address common misunderstandings and questions in the next two chapters. For others, this study may have inspired you. But while it is exciting to take hold of God's Word and His will on this subject, don't run out and try to become a millionaire tomorrow! It takes time and consistent walking in God's wisdom to prosper in His way. Be patient, and continue to study and act upon His Word.

Second, take time to complete this workbook. In the course of our study, we will find out how to prosper God's way. God wants you to not only understand His will, but to also understand His way of walking in His will. Don't be discouraged if you are struggling or have struggled in this area. The first step toward walking in all God has for you is to obtain the knowledge of His will. Take one step at a time, and God will teach you how to profit!

C. PERSONAL APPLICATION

Why not take a moment to pray? A prayer like this from your heart will help to set you on the right course for this study:

Dear God, I am so thankful for Your Word. It is the Truth. Your Word reveals Your will, and I am so grateful that I am beginning to get a better working knowledge of Your plan for my prosperity. I ask You, Father, to continue to fill me with the knowledge of Your will in all wisdom and spiritual understanding, that I may walk in a manner worthy of You, being fruitful in every good work. I thank You for leading me by Your Word and by Your Spirit into prosperous living. In Jesus' name. Amen.

CHAPTER TWO

"YEAH, BUT..."
A LOOK AT COMMON MISUNDERSTANDINGS ABOUT PROSPEROUS LIVING

The subject of prosperity has raised no small stir among believers of all denominations. This is so unfortunate, because something God meant to be a blessing to believers and to the kingdom of God has become a divisive issue. Those who embrace God's will to prosper have been called the "name-it-and-claim-it bunch," the "health-and-wealth believers" or the "hundredfold-heresy Christians." The result has been much misunderstanding about this issue. There has been confusion about several familiar verses of Scripture, as well as the prosperity message as a whole.

Our goal in this chapter is to examine several verses of Scripture that have seemingly caused misunderstanding. We will look at answers to these questions: •Didn't Jesus warn against serving both God and money? •Isn't money the root of all evil? •Doesn't the Bible say it's impossible for a rich man to enter into the kingdom of God? •Didn't Jesus say the poor will be with us always? •Isn't God sovereign when it comes to prospering people? •Aren't poverty and lack the signs of true spiritual humility? •Doesn't the Bible tell us to desire neither poverty nor riches?

So, is the prosperity message a false teaching, or is it God's will? Our doctrine should not be based upon traditions, excess, pious thinking or notions of false humility. In this study, we will examine in some detail numerous Scriptures to see what the Bible does, in fact, teach. Remember, it is important to rightly divide the Word of God. Anyone can take an isolated verse to make it say anything. So we want to look at several verses of Scripture and by the mouth of two or three witnesses let our doctrine be established.

The best way to approach this study is much like the Bereans, as described in Acts 17:11: **These were more noble than those in Thessalonica, in that they received the word with all readiness of mind, and searched the scriptures daily, whether those things were so.** In other words, the Bereans didn't just take at face value what the apostle Paul or any other disciple said was the truth. They studied the Scriptures themselves to be sure what Paul said was true.

This is a good example to follow. Study your own Bible for yourself to be sure that what you hear is indeed the truth. We want you to become convinced of God's will on the subject of prosperity because you have searched the Scriptures in your own Bible! To do this objectively, you may have to take off your "traditional" ways of thinking. Remember, Jesus told His disciples that the "traditions of men" made the Word of God of no effect. (Matt. 15:6; Mark 7:13.)

Let's begin by looking at common misconceptions about prosperous living. As we study God's Word, keep an open mind and heart. Trust God through the Holy Spirit to lead you into all truth.

A. DIDN'T JESUS WARN AGAINST SERVING BOTH GOD AND MONEY?

This is true; Jesus did make that statement. But what did He mean by it? Did He mean you can't serve God and have money? Did He mean if you have money you can't serve God? What does it mean to serve money?

Actually, we find that Jesus is talking about "trust" in this Scripture. He is saying that you can't trust in both God and money; your trust must be in one or the other. Is it possible to trust God and still have money? Let's look at the Scriptures.

1. Matthew 6:24

    What two things did Jesus say you cannot serve simultaneously? _____
    _____

    Why is it impossible to serve both God and mammon, or money? _____
    _____

2. 1 Timothy 6:17

    What did the Holy Spirit, through the apostle Paul, tell those who are rich not to do? ___
    _____

    What do you think it means by "trusting in uncertain riches"? _____
    _____

We can see the same thought in both of these Scriptures — that we are to love God and to trust in Him. We are not to love money nor trust in it. It's impossible to love and trust in money and in God at the same time. But Jesus isn't saying that it's impossible to love and trust in God and still have money. Let's look at this in more detail as we study the next question.

B. ISN'T MONEY THE ROOT OF ALL EVIL?

1 Timothy 6:8-11,17-19

According to verse 10, what is the root of all evil — "money" or the "love of money"? _____
_____

What does verse 10 say about "coveting after money"? _____

_____

In verse 17, what did God say to rich people about "trust?" _____

_____

It's clear that money is not evil. Money is neutral. It's neither evil nor good. It's what we do with money that makes it evil or good. Money is simply a tool for doing good or evil. The main point of these passages is the condition of our heart. Is our heart loving and trusting in money, or loving and trusting in God?

C. DOESN'T THE BIBLE SAY IT IS IMPOSSIBLE FOR A RICH MAN TO ENTER INTO THE KINGDOM OF GOD?

This is one of those Scriptures that has tripped up believers for centuries! Was Jesus saying that rich people couldn't be saved? Was He telling us to avoid being rich? Let's look in detail at this passage.

1. Mark 10:17-27

    This is the story of the rich young ruler. Jesus loved this man. After a series of questions and answers, Jesus asked him to sell all he had and give it to the poor, then come and follow Him. The rich young ruler went away sad, for he had a great number of possessions but wouldn't part with them. He loved and trusted in his riches more than he loved Jesus.

    Following this story, what did Jesus say to His disciples in verses 23 and 24? _____

    _____

    _____

    Jesus was conveying the idea that it will be hard for rich people to stop trusting in their riches and to trust in Him. This isn't because God is unmerciful or unwilling for them to trust Him, but because a wealthy person grows accustomed to trusting in his own wealth for prestige, influence, status and purchasing power. This position in life can be very gratifying to the flesh, so it's difficult for some people to let go of it and to trust in God. Jesus is just stating a fact of human nature. It isn't impossible for a rich person to stop trusting in his own wealth and to follow Jesus, but it's more difficult for him than it would be for the person who has nothing to lose. This makes logical sense, because it's the nature of the flesh.

    What were Jesus and His disciples talking about in verses 25-27? _____

    _____

    _____

Some people think Jesus was referring to a geographical area called "the eye of a needle," which camels had difficulty passing through. Others believe Jesus was literally speaking of a needle and thread and of the impossible task of putting a camel through the eye of a needle.

In verse 27, Jesus said, With men it is impossible, but not with God: for with God all things are possible. What do you think He meant? _____

_____

Perhaps Jesus was telling the disciples that men's ways of obtaining salvation through money, influence and power were impossible, but God's way of obtaining salvation through faith by grace was possible. In other words, the rich and the poor alike must approach God the same way — on His terms. When we do things God's way, nothing is impossible!

Clearly, the point of this passage is not that it's wrong to be rich, but that it's wrong to "trust in riches." Let's look at several other Scriptures that convey the command not to trust in riches.

2. Psalm 49:6,7

    According to verse 6, what were these wealthy people doing? _____

    _____

    Could their money redeem anyone? _____

3. Psalm 52:7

    What did this ungodly man trust in? _____

    What did he not trust in? _____

    What did this lead him to do? _____

    _____

4. Psalm 62:10

    What are we not to trust in? _____

    What do you think it means to "set your heart upon" something? _____

    _____

5. Proverbs 11:28

    What happens to the person who trusts in his riches? _____

    _____

What happens to the righteous one who trusts in God? _____

_____

6.　Matthew 13:22

How do riches deceive people? _____

If a person was trusting in riches, could he be deceived by them? _____

_____

What does the deceitfulness of riches do to a person? _____

_____

Again, we see that when we trust in our riches rather than in God and in His Word, we can be deceived and sidetracked by the deceitful allure of money. The result is that the Word is choked in our lives and we become unfruitful.

7.　1 Timothy 6:17

What did the Holy Spirit, through the apostle Paul, warn rich people not to trust in?

_____

In your own words, state why you think Paul used the phrase "uncertain riches". _____
_____
_____

What are rich people told to trust in? _____

What does the living God give us? _____

_____

Why does God give us all things richly? _____

_____

God is not against us having nice things, being blessed richly or having wealth. In fact, we are told that God gives us all things richly so that we may enjoy them! What displeases God is when we trust in those riches rather than in Him.

8.　Proverbs 3:5,6

Who are we supposed to trust in? _____

What are we not supposed to trust in or lean on? _____

_____

If we trust God and acknowledge Him in all our ways, what will He do? _____
_____

Could He direct our steps into prosperity, which is obtained His way — for His purposes?
_____

Certainly He could! And that will be the subject of our study for much of this book.

D. DIDN'T JESUS SAY THE POOR WILL BE WITH US ALWAYS?

Yes, Jesus did say this, but what was He talking about? Did He mean to infer that, since we would always have the poor with us, we should not prosper? Many times people will use a statement like this to imply that since there will always be poor people, we should not prosper. Of course, this doesn't make any logical sense, for how can we help the poor unless we do prosper? Just because other people drop out of school before they graduate, should we drop out and not graduate? Just because other people don't fulfill their potential, should we not fulfill ours? Let's look at this verse of Scripture to see what Jesus was talking about.

1. Matthew 26:6-11 (see also John 12:1-8)

    What event preceded Jesus' statement about the poor? _____
    _____

    When Jesus said, Ye have the poor always with you, was He implying that Mary or His followers should be poor also? _____
    _____

    When Jesus mentioned the poor, did He include Himself as being a poor person? _____
    _____

    If Jesus had been so concerned about the poverty of the poor and the "wrongful" wealth of Mary, shouldn't He have rebuked Mary for "wasting" that very expensive perfume on Him?_____
    _____

    Who rebuked Mary for "wasting" that very expensive perfume? _____
    _____

    Did Judas care about the poor? _____
    _____

    Do you want to be in the same category of person as Judas? _____
    _____

Of course not! When Jesus said, Ye have the poor always with you, He was merely stating a fact of life. It would be similar to us saying, "You have the sick always with you," or

"You have unbelievers always with you." These are true statements. Though this is not God's will or God's highest and best, it is a fact nonetheless.

2. Luke 4:18

What did Jesus come to preach to the poor? _____

What would good news be to the spiritually poor? _____
_____

What would good news be to the fiscally poor? _____
_____

Unfortunately, there are people who are spiritually and financially poor who will not receive or walk in the good news that Jesus came to bring to them. The result is that we will always have the poor, both spiritually and fiscally, with us. It isn't God's plan, but it is a fact.

E. ISN'T GOD SOVEREIGN WHEN IT COMES TO PROSPERING PEOPLE?

Does God sovereignly choose to prosper certain people? Does God in His sovereignty only allow "those He can trust" to be blessed with wealth? (If so, what does this say about those who aren't blessed with wealth — that God can't trust them?) In other words, does the Bible teach us that God has the prerogative to prosper some people while keeping others in humbler means?

Oftentimes, in the area of prosperity, people have the idea that it is somehow God's providential blessing for them to be closer to poverty than to prosperity. They have the notion that to be broke, and barely making ends meet, is a sign of spirituality and God's sovereign blessing upon their lives. Many have thought that God in His wisdom "picks" people to be economically lower, middle, or perhaps even upper class.

We certainly believe that God is Sovereign and Almighty. However, in doctrines where He has already stated His will in His Word, He will not violate that will by exercising His sovereignty. God will not contradict His own Word! If, according to His Word, He has given us His plan and His guidelines for our prosperity, then we have a responsibility to walk according to that plan. To the degree that we do, we will be blessed. To the degree that we don't, we will not be blessed.

As you study the Bible, you will see an "if/then" principle at work in the Word of God. *If* we walk according to His Word, *then* He blesses us in line with His promises to us. Actually, we will see from the Bible that God doesn't necessarily choose our lot in life — in large part, we do! Obviously, we don't have any choice over who our parents are and what country we are born in. But do you know what? If we will put God's Word to work in our lives, regardless of our gender, race or nationality, in due time God will lift us up to His plan for our prosperity! Our prosperity depends more upon us and our cooperating with God's laws and principles than we might realize. (We will look at our responsibility before God in later chapters in this workbook.)

Let's look at a few verses where God in His sovereignty has given us the choice whether or not to prosper.

1. Deuteronomy 30:15-19

    You will notice that, throughout the Word of God, in most matters God gives us the opportunity to choose. If things were left entirely up to His sovereignty, why would He give us any choice in matters?

    According to verses 15 and 19, what has God set before us? _____

    _____

    Did you know, the Hebrew word for "good" in this verse is also translated other places in the Bible as "prosperity?"

    Will God sovereignly choose for us? _____

    Who has the responsibility for making the choice? _____

2. Isaiah 1:19

    If we want to eat the "good of the land" — what must we do? _____

    _____

    We must be "willing and obedient" to what? _____

    Whose will is involved in our ability to "eat the good of the land" — God's or ours?

    _____

    How would you describe the "good of the land"? _____

    _____

F. AREN'T POVERTY AND LACK THE SIGNS OF TRUE SPIRITUAL HUMILITY?

The Bible actually teaches just the opposite. If poverty and lack were the ingredients for true humility, then how do these next Scriptures fit that picture?

1. Numbers 12:3

    What does this verse tell us about Moses? _____
    _____

    If poverty is the true sign of humility, then Moses must have been the poorest man to have ever lived! But there are no indications from the Word that Moses was poor. In fact, we see him grow up in Pharaoh's house — a house of wealth! But then when he had reached adulthood, he **refused to be called the son of Pharaoh's daughter; choosing rather to suffer affliction with the people of God, than to enjoy the pleasures of sin for a season; esteeming the reproach of Christ greater riches than the treasures in Egypt: for he had respect unto the recompence of the reward** (Heb. 11:24-26).

    Moses refused the world's wealth. But as we will see, God saw to it that he was prosperous! We see him, as the leader of Israel, giving Israel instructions on how to prosper in an incredible way in Exodus. If poverty was what pleased God, don't you think Moses of all leaders would have encouraged his followers to walk in this type of humility and meekness? Moses was God's chosen man! We would expect him to demonstrate by his own life and to instruct the children of Israel to walk in line with God's will. If poverty was a sign of true spiritual humility, then we should see Moses, of all men, demonstrating and teaching this to the Israelites.

    Let's look at the life of Moses, this humble servant of God.

    Exodus 3:21,22; 12:35,36

    What did the Lord, through Moses, tell the Israelites to borrow from the Egyptians?

    _____

    JEWELS: The Hebrew word for "jewels" is *keliy* (pronounced *kel-ee'*), which means any apparatus as an implement, utensil, dress, vessel, weapon, jewel, furniture, stuff, thing.[1]

    What happened in chapter 12, verses 35 and 36? _____
    _____

    Do you see God prospering the Israelites? _____

    Do you see Moses in full support of this prosperity? _____

    Exodus 35:4-29; 36:3-7

    We see no "doctrine of lack" in Moses' command to Israel, and we see no evidence of poverty among the Israelites! What type of offerings did they bring? _____
    _____

The Israelites were so wealthy and generous that Moses had to take drastic measures in chapter 36, verses 5-7. What did Moses do? _____

_____

When was the last time you were supporting a church or a ministry where the leadership asked you to stop bringing your offerings because they had too much?_____

_____

If poverty and lack were a part of God's plan, could there ever be an offering as is described in Exodus 36:3-7? _____

2. Psalm 84:11

If we walk uprightly before the Lord, are we promised poverty and lack?_____

_____

What are we promised? _____

3. Proverbs 22:4

What do humility and the fear of the Lord produce in a person's life? _____

If true humility meant one was to be poor, could this verse be true?_____

4. Matthew 5:5

Will meek or humble ones inherit poverty and lack? _____

What will they inherit? _____

G. DOESN'T THE BIBLE TELL US TO DESIRE NEITHER POVERTY NOR RICHES?

Proverbs 30:1-9

What did Agur say about poverty and riches in verses 8 and 9? _____

_____

At first glance, his words sound noble indeed! In verse 9, we see him insinuating that a person who had riches and wealth could deny the Lord and walk away from following Him. Although in some cases this may be true, we see many examples of Bible personalities who were rich and wealthy and still had a very close relationship with the Lord. We have already studied many of these in this workbook.

In verses 1 and 2, how does Agur describe himself? _____

_____

If a person described himself as brutish, without understanding, lacking wisdom and not knowing the holy God, then it makes sense that if this type of person were to obtain great riches and wealth, he or she could deny the Lord. For a person of this character, perhaps riches and wealth would not be in their best interest.

Are you brutish? Do you lack understanding, wisdom and knowledge of the holy God?

_____

H. PERSONAL APPLICATION

Before your study in this chapter, which of these common misunderstandings were confusing to you? Are any of them still confusing to you? If so, which ones?

Take time to go back over the Scriptures and ask the Holy Spirit for revelation on any passages that are difficult for you to understand.

CHAPTER THREE

"WHAT ABOUT...?"
A LOOK AT COMMON QUESTIONS ABOUT
PROSPEROUS LIVING

In addition to common misunderstandings, people have general questions concerning this subject of prosperous living. For centuries, the religious traditions of men, as well as the devil's own lies, have kept Christians living below God's best for them. It takes time to renew your mind to the Word of God on this subject. Although we may be answering some of your questions and bringing God's light to areas that you may not have considered before, perhaps we are raising several new questions as well. In this chapter, we will take a few moments to look at some of the more common questions people have about prosperity.

Many good questions have been raised, such as: • Isn't the prosperity message just a carnal "get-rich-quick" scheme? • Isn't prosperity a sign of being worldly? • Why should I prosper when half the world lives in poverty? • Wouldn't too much prosperity tempt me to fall away from the Lord? • Isn't God's main concern our spiritual prosperity?

These are legitimate questions which we want to look at in further detail.

A. ISN'T THE PROSPERITY MESSAGE JUST A CARNAL "GET-RICH-QUICK" SCHEME?

Unfortunately, some preachers, as well as many believers, have made the prosperity message sound like a "get-rich-quick" scheme. There have been insincere sermons, deceptive appeals for money and "pie-in-the-sky" messages which have deluded some into thinking that God's will for prosperity is a carnal, money-making scheme. Some teaching along this line make God sound like Tinkerbell — if we will push the right buttons, God will sprinkle "magic dust" on our bank accounts and checkbooks whenever we need cash. This couldn't be farther from the truth! The Bible doesn't teach it, and this kind of thinking is ungodly. God is opposed to deception, trickery, con artistry and tainted money schemes. He warns us to avoid "filthy lucre," when money is gotten by deception and by ungodly means. (1 Tim. 3:3; 1 Peter 5:2.)

On the other hand, don't misunderstand what we are saying. God can certainly move in a miraculous way in your finances. He can lead you into employment or into a business venture that can be very profitable for you. There are many good, upright and honest Christian men and women who have exercised God's wisdom in business, and some have received the knowledge of witty inventions. These believers have prospered in such a way that it almost seemed they "got rich quick," yet they were inspired and led by God.

In the course of your lifetime, there will be many opportunities that come your way. You must exercise wisdom and discernment to tell the difference between the good and the bad, between what God is leading you into and what your carnal nature wants to pursue.

Perhaps you have had some opportunities which have led you to experience the disappointment of a business venture that went sour. It may not be God's best plan, but as the saying goes, experience is a good teacher! Don't allow yourself to be condemned about past failures. Pick yourself up and dust yourself off. Use experiences of failure as your education for the future, then continue to move on with God.

In this section, let's see what God's Word says about how to differentiate between a carnal, "get-rich-quick" scheme, and when God Himself is teaching you to profit.

1. Proverbs 13:11

   Wealth gotten by "vanity" does what?_____

   _____

   The Amplified Bible makes the word *vanity* in this verse a little clearer. It reads like this: **Wealth [not earned but] won in haste or unjustly or from the production of things for vain or detrimental use [such riches] will dwindle away, but he who gathers little by little will increase [his riches].**

   What happens to the wealth of the person who earns his money little by little through labor? _____

2. Proverbs 20:21

   What is the end result of "get-rich-quick" schemes? _____

   _____

3. Proverbs 21:5

   What do those who are hasty receive? _____

   What do those who are diligent receive? _____

4. Proverbs 28:20

   What happens to a faithful man? _____

What does this tell us about those who "make haste to be rich"?_____

_____

The idea of "innocent" in this verse is brought out in *The Amplified Bible,* where it says, **A faithful man shall abound with blessings, but he who makes haste to be rich [at any cost] shall not go unpunished.**

5. Proverbs 28:22

How is "he who hastens to be rich" described? _____

_____

What will come upon him? _____

B. ISN'T PROSPERITY A SIGN OF BEING WORLDLY?

It certainly can be, but it doesn't necessarily have to be. If by "worldly" we mean a person who is caught up with **the lust of the flesh, and the lust of the eyes, and the pride of life** (1 John 2:16), yes, a person can acquire riches and wealth simply to satisfy his carnal nature.

It's true that those who are wealthy face certain "worldly" temptations which those who are poor do not. However, at the same time, a poor person can be tempted just as much as a wealthy person can with certain "worldly" things, such as greed and covetousness. In some cases, a poor person may be even more tempted to lust after something he is unable to obtain than a rich person would be. Usually, those who don't have money spend more time thinking about how to get money and spend it than those who already have it.

Whether rich or poor, the real issue is the heart. In the Bible we see examples of believers who show us it is possible to be prosperous while at the same time maintain a right heart. In the Bible we see that God's people can prosper financially, have integrity and sincere motives, and be godly witnesses. Prosperity in and of itself is no sign of being worldly, just as poverty is no sign of being spiritual. A poverty-stricken person can be just as worldly as a Christian who is a multimillionaire. Worldliness is a matter of the heart. When someone isn't yielding to God, but rather to the lust of the flesh and of the eyes and the pride of life, this is worldliness.

1. 1 John 2:15-17

What three worldly things are not of the Father?_____

_____

_____

2. 1 Timothy 6:8-12

What are we to be content with? _____
_____

What temptations are faced by those who desire to be wealthy? _____
_____

What is the root of all evil — "money" or the "love of money"? _____

Which are we to flee — "money" or the "love of money"? _____
_____

What are we to follow? _____
_____

Do you think it's possible to follow after these things while being wealthy? _____
_____

C. WHY SHOULD I PROSPER IF OVER HALF THE WORLD LIVES IN POVERTY?

For one thing, you would never be able to help other people out of their poverty if you are entrenched in poverty yourself.

Many Christians are so focused on meeting the needs of their own families that they don't have much left to give to others. One great reason for sincere Christians to desire abundant prosperity is so that they have surplus wealth to give to others in need. Just because over half the world is in a poverty-stricken condition is no reason for believers to be poor.

Think of it this way: if half the population were going to hell, would you feel bad about going to heaven? Of course not. In fact, with your knowledge of how to get to heaven, you would have more motivation to help others avoid hell and go to heaven with you! The same is true about prosperity.

D. WOULDN'T TOO MUCH MONEY TEMPT ME TO FALL AWAY FROM THE LORD?

This is possible, but it depends upon what type of heart you have. Remember Agur from Proverbs 30 which we studied in our previous chapter? Having too much money probably wouldn't tempt you to fall away from the Lord anymore than not having enough money would. It's a matter of your heart being in the right place. By making money your idol, you could fall away from the Lord. But that's true about anything we might put in place of God. Hopefully, as a believer, you have developed a strong relationship with the Lord so that His prospering you would only cause you to give thanks and praise to Him for His abundant blessings. Then you would be motivated to give more and more to the work of the Gospel all around the world.

Let's look at this question in light of human relationships: Would too much money cause you to "fall away" from your spouse or close friend? Probably not. In fact, in many cases it's a lack of money that creates problems in relationships. But really, this issue is a matter of the heart that Jesus addressed in the parable of the sower. Let's look at it.

Mark 4:3-10,13-20

In this parable Jesus describes the Word being sown in four different types of soil, or heart conditions.

In verses 18 and 19, what three things did Jesus say choked the Word which these believers had heard?_____

_____

Why do you think riches can be deceitful? _____

_____

How do you think that can affect your relationship with the Lord?_____

_____

_____

E. ISN'T GOD'S MAIN CONCERN OUR SPIRITUAL PROSPERITY?

Of course it is, but that doesn't mean He isn't concerned with our material and financial needs as well. If God were only concerned with our spiritual needs, why does He address our material and financial needs in so many Bible passages? What is God telling us in this passage about our material and financial needs?

1. Matthew 6:25-33

   Is God aware of our needs? (v. 32.) _____

   What does He promise to do about our needs? (vv. 26,30,33.)_____

   _____

   _____

   We are not to be anxious or worried about our needs; so what are we to do? _____

   _____

   _____

2. 3 John 2

What three things did the Holy Spirit, through the apostle John, tell us He desired for us?

_____

_____

From this verse, can you see that God desires our "spiritual prosperity"? _____

Is "spiritual prosperity" the only thing He wants for us?_____

To what degree does God want us to "prosper and be in health"?_____

_____

We can see that God places financial prosperity and success on the same plane as our spiritual prosperity and our physical health. He wants us to prosper equally in all three areas of our lives!

Are you convinced yet? Prosperity is God's idea! Are you getting a vision for being blessed and being a blessing to others?

F. PERSONAL APPLICATION

Hopefully, this chapter has helped answer some of the common questions people have when it comes to the subject of prosperity.

Before moving on to the next chapter, why don't you take a moment to pray? Ask God to fill you with the knowledge of His will for your prosperity and the wisdom of His way so you will walk in all that is available to you. You may want to pray a prayer like this aloud from your heart:

> Dear Father, I thank You for illuminating the eyes of my heart and for already answering many of the questions I have had about prosperity. I ask You to fill me with the knowledge of Your will concerning my prosperity. I ask for Your grace to help where I need to change my thinking and for revelation as I study Your Word on this subject.
>
> Give me the wisdom I need to walk in Your will, Father, and give me Your grace to help where I need to change my behavior. I will be a doer of Your Word and not a hearer only. I am trusting You as I renew my mind to Your written Word and as I am led by the Holy Spirit.
>
> In the name of Jesus Christ, I believe that my life will be transformed in this area, that I will walk in new levels of prosperity, that I will experience the reality of prosperous living. I believe I will be blessed with new levels of wealth, and I commit myself to be used by You, Father, to give greater amounts of money to Your work all around the world. In Jesus' name. Amen.

CHAPTER FOUR

"THE MOTIVE QUESTION" WHY DO YOU WANT TO PROSPER?

Let's address the motive question.

What are your motives for desiring prosperity? This is an important question. Is it so you can impress your family and friends? Is it so you can sit back and enjoy a life of luxury? Is it just so you can get out of debt and live a comfortable life? Is it so you can give more money to your local church and to the work of the Gospel around the world? Is it so you can bring greater glory to God and His goodness?

Many of those who are opposed to what we call the "prosperity message" have been critical of Christians who have pursued prosperity for selfish, carnal and greedy reasons. They have been suspicious of believers with the wrong motives, who get excited about their prosperity and wealth, but don't get as excited about serving God, giving to others, or living holy lives. We have to agree with the critics: this is a contradiction. Unfortunately, many well-meaning but misguided people have been shipwrecked in their faith because they jumped on the "prosperity bandwagon" without ever really taking a look at the condition of their heart.

God's number-one concern is the condition of your heart! Before we continue any further with our study of prosperous living, let's take a moment to locate the condition of our heart, our motives for desiring prosperity and God's purpose in providing it for us.

The purpose of this book isn't to get you all "hyped up" about prosperity to the detriment of your spiritual life with God. You need a solid personal relationship with God through Jesus Christ, built upon the written Word of God. Jesus needs to be the Lord of your life — not just in theory — but in reality! Yes, there is a truth that the Body of Christ needs to hear concerning God's will for our prosperity. But there is a greater truth that needs to be discussed first: the importance of having a heart that's totally committed to and sold out for Jesus Christ and the Gospel. Even if it meant that there was no such thing as the "prosperity message" and that you would have to live on bread crumbs for the rest of your life here on planet Earth!

With this in mind, let's take a look at what the Bible tells us about these matters of the heart.

A. DO YOU HAVE THE RIGHT FOUNDATION? — A MATTER OF THE HEART

What do you love? This is a foundational question. In talking about heart matters, we must talk about the things we love in our heart. In a previous chapter, we studied the fact that it is possible to love God and have money. In this section, we want to take a closer look at the idea of loving God and the things of God, instead of loving money.

1. What do you love in your heart?

    a. Deuteronomy 6:5; Matthew 22:37; Mark 12:30; Luke 10:27

        Who are we to love? _____

        How are we to love God? _____

        Describe this type of love. _____

        _____

        Do you love God like this? _____

    b. Psalm 119:14,97,127,162

        What are we to love more than we love riches, gold and great spoil? _____

        _____

    c. 1 Timothy 6:9,10

        What are we not to love? _____

        What is the "love of money"? _____

        If a person covets after money, what is the result?_____

        _____

        According to these verses, what are some of the pitfalls of loving money and being rich? _____

        _____

    d. Mark 8:36

        In your own words, describe the phrase "gain the whole world." _____

        _____

        What is the answer to this question Jesus posed? _____

        _____

Can you see that in our heart we ought to love God and His Word more than anything else? Being wealthy, having riches and gaining the whole world is not worth a thing if in the process or in the end we lose our own souls! God cares about our heart, and He wants our heart to be in love with Him — not money!

2. Is Jesus the Lord of your heart?

   a. Romans 10:9

      In order to be saved, what must we call Jesus? _____

      When we call Jesus our Lord, what are we saying? _____

      When I think about Jesus being the Lord of my life, I always picture Him sitting in the driver's seat, behind the steering wheel of my life. In other words, He calls the shots and directs my life. I am submitted to His leadership in my life. I seek His will and follow His lead. I inquire of Him and His will in every area of my life. When His will is different than what I want to do, if He is truly my Lord, I must submit my desire and follow His will. For Jesus to be the Lord of our lives is more than just a clichè that we repeat. It is a vital, daily reality.

      Is Jesus truly the Lord of your life? _____

      Are there any areas of your life where He is not the Lord? _____

      If so, you must deal with these areas if you truly want to prosper in life. What areas are you now turning over to His lordship? _____

   b. Luke 6:46-49

      Jesus was not pleased with those who called Him Lord but would not do the things He said. What is He saying to us about true lordship in this passage? _____
      _____

3. How is your heart prospering?

   a. Proverbs 4:23

      What are we to do with our heart? _____
      _____

      What comes out of our heart? _____

      Much could be said about this verse, but in the context of our subject — prosperous living — it is important that we guard our heart. It is from our heart that the very issues of life flow. Our inner life does affect our outer life. The prosperity of our heart, or inner life, is proportionate to the prosperity of our outer life.

How is your inner life? Are you enjoying fellowship with the Lord through His Word and by His Spirit? Is your thought life managed? Is peace ruling in your heart? You must take some time to examine your life to be sure prosperous living is happening internally before you spend too much time believing God for prosperous living externally! Let's look at a few verses along this line.

b. Deuteronomy 29:9

To prosper in all that we do, what is the first priority? _____

c. Joshua 1:7,8

To prosper and have good success, what are we to meditate on in our heart, to speak out of our mouth and to do with our actions? _____

d. Psalm 1:2,3

Describe the inner life of the person who prospers in whatever he does. _____

e. Matthew 6:19-21,33

Jesus said, **For where your treasure is, there will your heart be also** (v. 21). In your own words, what did He mean by this? _____

What does God promise to those who seek Him first? _____

f. 3 John 2

God wants us to prosper externally to the degree that we are prospering where?
_____

B. ARE YOU HAPPY WITH WHAT YOU HAVE? — A MATTER OF CONTENTMENT

1. Philippians 4:11-13

What had Paul learned to be? _____
_____

What type of circumstances had he experienced? _____
_____

2. 1 Timothy 6:6-8

    Godliness with _____ equals great gain.

    "Great gain" implies prosperity, so being content is a form of prosperity!

    We should be content if we have what two things?

    _____   _____

3. Hebrews 13:5

    What is our conversation (manner of life) to be without? _____
    _____

    What type of heart attitude are we to have with the things we have and with the knowledge that Jesus will never leave us nor forsake us? _____

    In your own words, describe contentment. _____
    _____
    _____

CONTENT: We see two Greek words translated as "content." They are *autarkes* (pronounced *ow-tar'-kace*),[1] which means to be contented with one's lot, with one's means, though the slenderest; and *arkeo* (pronounced *ar-keh'-o*),[2] which means to be content, be sufficient, be enough, and to suffice.

Sometimes in dealing with this subject of contentment, Christians have gotten the idea that to be content means to have a fatalistic view of life. We get a "whatever will be, will be" attitude, or a "this is my lot in life, so I might as well learn to live with it" mentality. But this isn't what contentment means. It is possible to be content and thankful with your lot in life, yet at the same time be believing God and what His Word says about your prosperity. To be content doesn't mean to put your faith on hold or to cast away your confidence for a more prosperous future; it simply means to be thankful and at peace with where you are.

C. ARE YOUR MOTIVES PURE? — A MATTER OF GREED AND COVETOUSNESS

We are warned over and over in God's Word to avoid greed and covetousness. When studying these subjects of prosperity and prosperous living, one area we want to take a look at is how to discern between God's will for our prosperity and our own evil desire for greed and covetousness. First, let's define our terms.

GREEDY: The Greek word for "greedy" is *aischrokerdes* (pronounced *ahee-skhrok-er-dace'*).[3] It means eager for base gain or greedy for money. It is also translated as the phrase, "filthy lucre," which we find in the New Testament. One Hebrew word translated "greedy" is *batsa`* (pronounced *baw-tsah'*).[4] It means to plunder, to gain greedily, to be given to covetousness, to be covetous.

COVETOUSNESS: The Greek word for "covetousness" is *pleonexia* (pronounced *pleh-on-ex-ee'-ah*), which means a greedy desire to have more.[5] There is also a Hebrew word *betsa`* (pronounced *beh'-tsah*), which means to have an unjust gain, and dishonest gain.[6]

In other words, to be greedy or covetous is to be eager for gain and for money by wrongful, unrighteous, unethical or violent means. To obtain wealth at any cost — for selfish reasons, by using ungodly means, by stepping on whomever might be in the way — is a sure sign of greed and covetousness. Let's look at the Scriptures.

1. Psalm 119:36

    What are we to incline our hearts unto? _____

    What are we to stay away from? _____

2. Proverbs 28:16

    What is promised to "he that hateth covetousness"? _____

3. Ezekiel 33:31

    God is talking about people who say they love Him; but in looking at their hearts, what does He see? _____

4. Luke 12:15-21

    What does this passage tell us about our love for possessing things? _____
    _____

    How many times in this passage did the rich man use the pronoun *I* or *my*? _____

    In verse 21, there is a summary description of a covetous person; what is the summary?
    _____

    God summarizes the rich man's wrong motive and wrong use of money. What does He say about this man's heart and wealth in relation to God and God's kingdom? _____
    _____

    We are to take heed and beware of what? _____

What does a man's life not consist of? _____
_____

Describe the life of this covetous person. _____
_____
_____

If we are rich toward God, can we avoid being covetous? _____

5. Romans 1:28-32; 1 Corinthians 5:9-13; 6:9,10; Ephesians 5:1-7; Colossians 3:5; 2 Timothy 3:1-5; 2 Peter 2:10-15

   In these passages, we see God's hatred for covetousness in the lives of believers and unbelievers alike. After reading these passages, summarize in a sentence or two the type of person who is covetous. _____
   _____
   _____

6. Exodus 18:21; 1 Thessalonians 2:4,5; 1 Timothy 3:2-12

   God has certain qualifications for those who will be His leaders. Among these requirements, what is the one thing they must not be? _Covetous_____

7. Proverbs 1:19; 15:27

   What does greed do to a person? _It takes away from a person's life & brings destruction_

D. WHY DO YOU WANT TO PROSPER? — A MATTER OF PURPOSE

By now, maybe you are having second thoughts about prospering at all. When looking at these heart issues, we are challenged to the core of our being, and our motives are exposed. This isn't all bad, especially if in the light of God's Word we make the necessary corrections. So we trust that your heart has made any necessary adjustments and that your purpose for prosperity is becoming clearer and purer.

Let's take a look at this final motive issue: *why do we want to prosper?* Maybe a better way to say it would be, *why does God want us to prosper?* I believe there are two main reasons we should want to prosper, and these are the two main reasons God wants us to prosper.

First, God loves you, and He wants you to be blessed. He wants to be a blessing to you! He wants your needs and the desires of your heart to be met. He doesn't want His children to experience lack in any area of life. If Jesus doesn't return in your lifetime, He wants you to be able to leave an inheritance for your children and for your children's children. (Prov. 13:22.)

He wants you and your family to be blessed! We saw evidence of this through the Abrahamic Covenant, and we are still heirs of this covenant. Like any good father, God wants His children to be blessed with prosperity!

Second, God loves others, and He wants to bless them through you. You can be a blessing to a fellow Christian in need. You can be a blessing to those who are poor. You can be a blessing to lost humanity. God's heart is to reach those who are lost and separated from Him and are on their way to hell. He wants to use His Body, His children, to reach these lost souls. God's desire is to reap a worldwide harvest of souls. He wants His Covenant to be established around the world. So one of the main purposes for our prosperity is to take the Gospel of the Lord Jesus Christ all around the world. It is a fact: the more money and wealth you have, the more money you will be able to give to God's works around the world!

So, we could put it this way: God wants to establish His covenant to you and through you.

Let's look at these two reasons for prosperity.

1. God wants to establish His Covenant *to* you:

    God loves you! You are His child, and He wants His children to be taken care of. We have already looked at numerous Scriptures that should have convinced you that God wants you to be blessed and prosperous. If necessary, take a moment to review some of the earlier chapters. Let's look at more Scripture along this line.

    a. 1 Timothy 6:17,18

        According to this passage, God admonishes the rich of this world in a few areas. He tells them not to be high-minded (snooty) or to trust in uncertain riches, but to trust in the living God. He tells them to do good, to be rich in good works, to be ready to distribute and to give their wealth to others.

        In verse 17, God is described as a God Who gives us richly all things; for what purpose? _____

        Describe what "giveth us richly all things to enjoy" would mean in your life. _____
        _____

    b. Proverbs 10:22

        What is it that makes us rich? _____

        What do you think "He adds no sorrow with it" means? _____

        It is the blessing of God that makes you rich! God wants you to be rich without apology, without heartache, without guilt and without your having to defend your right to be prosperous. It is God's blessing that makes His children rich!

2. God wants to establish His Covenant *through* you:

   a. Deuteronomy 8:7-18

   In verses 7-16, we see God's blessing upon His people. God wanted to establish His Covenant with the Israelites, and the result was great prosperity and blessings in their lives. Describe the prosperity of God's people. _____

   In verses 17 and 18, God wants us to be sure we remember something very important: Who gives us the power to get wealth? _____

   Why does He give us this power? _____

   Describe what this means. _____

   ESTABLISH HIS COVENANT: On one hand, we see God establishing, and fulfilling the covenants He had with Abraham and Moses as He blessed the Israelites. On the other hand, we can see a New Testament application for this phrase. God gives us the power to obtain wealth under the New Covenant so that His Covenant can be established in the lives of countless lost people who need the saving knowledge of Jesus Christ. We can establish His Covenant around the world by giving a percentage of our wealth to churches, ministries, missionaries and other works of the Gospel.

   b. James 5:1-7

   The rich men have heaped treasures for what time period? _____

   According to verses 4 and 5, what was the error of the rich man? _____

   What should the rich man have done with his wealth? _____

   According to verse 4, in the day in which we live, who are the endtime harvest laborers? _____

   If you were to paraphrase this passage in modern terms, how would you explain it?
   _____

   I believe this passage is a clear picture of the endtime harvest. It's also an admonishment to those who are rich: that they use their wealth to establish God's Covenant in the earth! We see in verse 4 a picture of laborers who are working in the fields. This includes Gospel workers like pastors, evangelists, missionaries and other Christians who are laboring on mission fields, in churches and among the lost at home and abroad. But these laborers of the Gospel are not being compensated by those who are wealthy — those who live in pleasure back at home and lack for nothing. These workers cry out to God about their lack of wages, their lack of necessary funds to do the work of the harvest. God hears them and encourages them to be patient, for their work is almost done. There are just a few more souls to reap — the precious fruit of the earth; then Jesus will return! This is an encouragement to those who are working in the Gospel fields, but it is an indictment against those who are wealthy and not fully supporting the Gospel workers like they should! God gives us the power to get wealth to establish His Covenant, which means taking care of His workers in the field.

God gives us the power to get wealth for a reason — to establish His Covenant — to preach the Gospel to the ends of the earth!

Has this chapter stirred you to examine yourself? To rethink your motives? To check your own heart? If so, good! We thoroughly believe that God wants His children to be blessed with abundant prosperity. Christians, who have the right motives, who have hearts that are pure and focused on godly purposes, ought to be the most blessed people in the world!

E. PERSONAL APPLICATION

Be as honest as you can when answering these questions:

1. Heart matters:

    Do you love God with all your heart?

    Do you love God and His Word more than money?

    Do you think you love money?

    Is Jesus Christ the Lord of your heart and your lifestyle?

    Is your spiritual life prospering?

2. Contentment matters:

    Have you learned to be content with the things you have?

    Have you learned how to be content, while at the same time by faith you are expecting more from God?

3. Greed and covetousness matters:

    Are you willing to prosper through unjust, unethical, questionable or violent means?

    Do you find yourself craving, lusting or being greedy for things?

Do you get jealous or envious when others are blessed with things?

Are you rich toward God?

4. Purpose matters:

    Do you have a difficult time believing that God wants you to be rich, simply because He loves you and wants you to enjoy life?

    Do you see that we are not to be rich for merely selfish reasons and that we are to be generous givers in establishing His Covenant around the world?

    How are you using the wealth you currently have to establish God's Covenant?

    Are you a generous, cheerful giver?

It would be wise for you to review the Scriptures in this chapter to be sure you have the right motives and purpose as we continue in our study of prosperity.

CHAPTER FIVE

"IN THE BEGINNING..."
PROSPEROUS LIVING FROM COVER TO COVER

As we study the Bible from Genesis to Revelation, we see God's provision for the wealth and prosperity of His people. From the Garden of Eden right on through to our eternal home in heaven, we see God's desire for the prosperity of His children. In this chapter, we will look at God's original plan for man's prosperity. We will look at His Covenant with man, which included prosperous living. And we will look at the personal accounts of prosperity in the lives of those who served God in both the Old and New Testaments.

A. PROSPERITY IS A PART OF GOD'S ORIGINAL PLAN

1. Genesis 1:26-31

    According to verses 26 and 28-30, when God created mankind, what type of authority did He delegate to man? _____

    _____

    What type of provision did God make for mankind? _____

    _____

    Do you see God withholding from man or desiring lack in any part of his life? _____

    According to verse 28, God's first command was for man to do what?_____

    _____

We can see that God's original intention for man was full of life, health, provision and prosperity exceeding and abundant! We can obviously see in our day and age that mankind is not walking in this type of life in great measure. So what happened? When did poverty and lack enter the human race? Poverty, sickness and death entered when sin entered! Let's take a look at this subject.

2. Genesis 2:15-17

    According to verse 17, what did God tell Adam would happen if he ate of the tree of the knowledge of good and evil?_____

    _____

In other words, if Adam ate of this tree, death would be the result. Death would enter the human race the moment Adam ate of the tree of the knowledge of good and evil. Let's see what Adam did with God's command.

3. Genesis 3:1-6

    In verse 4, what did the serpent (Satan) say concerning God's words to Adam? _____
    _____

    What happened in verse 5? _____
    _____

Adam and his wife, Eve, disobeyed God's command, and they ate of the forbidden tree. At that moment, death entered the human race. Adam and Eve did not die physically at that moment; in fact, Adam lived to be 930 years old! But they died spiritually when they sinned by disobeying God's command. The moment they ate of the tree, they died spiritually and were separated from God. When this happened, death was passed on to the rest of humanity. Let's look at this spiritual law as it is revealed in the New Testament.

4. Romans 5:12

    How did sin enter the world? _____

    What was the result of sin? _____

    To whom did death pass?_____

Let's discuss the subject of death. There are three types of death described in the Bible: spiritual death (Gen. 2:17; 3:6-24), physical death (Gen. 5:5), and the second death (Rev. 20:11-15). Sin brought all types of death into the world. Until sin entered, there was nothing but abundant life. Let's look at a few aspects of death.

We know that spiritual death is not cessation of being, but rather the separation from God. In physical death, our physical body quits functioning. At that time, our spirit leaves our body and goes to be with the Lord (2 Cor. 5:1-8). (Concerning physical death, it was never in God's original plan that our physical body die. If Adam had not sinned, his body would never have died because he was created in God's image. Death was not a part of God's original plan; mortality was not a part of God's original design for man's body!)

We know that sin brought death, so we want to take a moment to examine what this means.

Sin brought spiritual death as well as physical death. By thinking about the dimension of physical death, we can actually conclude that sin also brought sickness and poverty along with it for these reasons. Sickness and poverty are nothing more than pre-death conditions. In other words, sickness and poverty are precursors to death.

Sickness is a pre-death condition. If a person gets enough sickness or disease in his body, it will lead to death. Sickness and disease are a form of death in its early stages.[1]

Poverty is also a pre-death condition. If a person is starved for food, water, shelter and the comforts of life long enough, that will lead to death. We have seen what famine does to a nation. Famine is poverty in its severest form, and it certainly is not a blessing from God! Poverty was never part of God's original plan. But when sin entered the world, death came, too; and with death came poverty in all its various forms.

B. PROSPERITY IS A PART OF GOD'S COVENANTS WITH MAN

Did you know that when sin and death entered the human race God had a plan for restoring man? God was interested in helping mankind overcome the effects of sin and death. He wanted to restore the relationship He had with man, and He wanted His people to once again walk in the blessings of His plan.

To do this, God established agreements, or covenants, with man. In fact, we see throughout the Word of God that He made several different covenants with His people. We aren't going to study this in detail, but in the Bible we can see some of the major covenants God made with man. There was the Adamic Covenant (Gen. 3:14-19,21), the Noahic Covenant (Gen. 6:18), the Abrahamic Covenant (Gen. 12:1-3; 15:18) (Gen. 17:1-8), (Gen. 17:1-8), the Mosaic Covenant (Ex. 24:7,8), the Davidic Covenant (2 Sam. 7:1-17) and the New Covenant (Matt. 26:28; 2 Cor. 3:6-18). Each covenant had terms of agreement. God established promises, conditions and agreements with His people. God's covenants were given to bless His people. God has always desired for His people to be blessed, and it was through a covenant relationship that He intended for them to be blessed.

Concerning the New Covenant as is found in the New Testament, we see in Hebrews 8:6 that, through Jesus Christ and His shed blood, we have been given "a new and better Covenant that was built upon better promises" than the Old Covenant. (The "Old Covenant" is a reference to the Mosaic Covenant in particular and other covenants in general.) If we, as New Testament believers, are under a "new and better Covenant," then it would be wise for us to find out about the Old Covenant. At least this will help us to see what God has improved upon! As we look at the Old Covenant, revealed in the Old Testament, we will be able to better understand our "new and better Covenant."

If when we study the Scriptures, we find that under the Old Covenant, God's people were blessed with prosperity — then we need to ask ourselves: Under our new and better Covenant, how much more does God want us, the Body of Christ, to be blessed with prosperity? In other words, if we can prove from the Bible that God's people in the Old Testament were blessed with wealth, riches, prosperity, treasures, substance and material blessings in great abundance — then to be consistent we must conclude that our "new and better Covenant" includes all of these — plus some! We may find that we have to expand our vision to line up with God's plan for prosperous living.

Hebrews 8:6

This verse tells us that Jesus is the Mediator of what type of covenant? _____
_____

This covenant is based upon what type of promises? _____

If our "better covenant with better promises" did not provide for our prosperity as did the Old Covenant, would it really be better?_____
_____

Therefore, if our New Covenant is a better covenant, based upon better promises — then we can be assured that if the Old Covenant promised and provided wealth and prosperity for the Jews — our "better covenant with better promises" would, at the very least, have the same promises for prosperity! And according to this verse, we should expect even better provision for prosperous living!

C. PROSPERITY IS REVEALED IN THE LIVES OF GOD'S PEOPLE

Let's take a look at prosperity in the Old Testament, under the Old Covenant, while keeping in mind that we are under a new and better Covenant.

Prosperous living is God's idea, and has been from the beginning! From the Garden of Eden, God's desire was that His children be blessed with abundance, that they be fruitful and multiply. We see evidence of God's blessing in the area of prosperity in the lives of numerous Old Testament saints: from Adam and Eve in the garden; to the patriarchs Abraham, Isaac, Jacob and Joseph; to Moses, Joshua and the children of Israel; to kings David, Solomon, Jehoshaphat and Hezekiah. Let's take some time to study the financial and material prosperity of these Old Testament believers.

1. The Blessing of Abraham:

   First, we want to look at a few New Testament passages which will help our study in the Old Testament.

   a. Galatians 3:13,14; 3:6-9; 3:26-29

      According to verse 13, what has Jesus redeemed us from? _____
      _____
      _____

      THE LAW: Under the Old Testament, "the Law" referred to the Pentateuch, the first five books of the Bible. The Law is summarized in Deuteronomy, chapters 28 and 29. In looking at the Law, we see that "the curse" for committing sin and breaking God's

Law was threefold: sickness, poverty, and death. When Jesus Christ hung on the cross, He redeemed (rescued) us from the curse of the Law — including death, sickness and poverty. (Some theologians teach that the "curse of the Law" here is only a reference to the curse of being under the Law; that is, as opposed to being under grace. Of course, being under the Law is a curse, but the Law clearly outlines the curses that come upon those who break God's Law.)

We can see from verse 13 that Jesus redeemed us *from* something; in verse 14 we can see what He redeemed us *into*.

According to verse 14, because of Jesus' death on the cross and by faith in Jesus Christ, what can now come on the Gentiles, or non-believers? _____
_____

To understand the "blessing of Abraham," we will study his life to see what this actually refers to. (Some theologians teach that the "blessing of Abraham" is a reference to God's pronouncement that Abraham was righteous by faith. Certainly, the ability to stand righteously before God through faith in Jesus Christ is a blessing, but we believe the Scriptures teach that the "blessing of Abraham" included righteousness by faith, as well as other elements. We will study these as we look into Abraham's life.)

What do verses 6-9 tell us about who will be "blessed with faithful Abraham"? _____
_____

In verses 26-29, it is even clearer that we New Testament believers are heirs of Abraham's blessing. If we belong to Christ — by our faith in Him (v. 26) — then whose seed are we?_____

We are heirs according to what? _____

What was the "promise" made to Abraham? What was the "blessing of Abraham"? If we can discover from a study of Abraham's life in the Old Testament just what the "promise" and the "blessing" are, then we know from the New Testament that, through our faith in Jesus Christ, we are heirs of this blessing.

Let's take a closer look at all that is meant by the "blessing of Abraham". To do so, we need to take a look at the life of this man Abraham, whom God called the "father of the faith".

b. Genesis 12:1-3

This is the first mention of God's promise of blessing to Abraham (or Abram). According to verses 2 and 3, what were included in God's blessing on Abraham? _____
_____
_____

We see that the "blessing of Abraham" included land that God had ordained for him, so Abraham was the first real-estate tycoon! This blessing also included national greatness and a great name. Abraham would be a blessing to others. Those who blessed him would be blessed by God; those who cursed him would be cursed by God. His family, as well as all families that came from him, would be blessed. (This is also a reference to the seed of the Messiah that was in him, and through Christ all families would be blessed eternally.)

c. Genesis 12:5; 13:1-6

What do these verses tell us about the material prosperity of Abram, or Abraham?
_____

According to chapter 13, verse 2, how is Abram described? _____
_____

Abram was rich with what? _____

Let's look at a few more verses of Scripture that paint a picture of Abraham's wealth.

d. Genesis 14:14

How many trained servants did Abram (Abraham) have? _____
_____

Would Abram have to be very rich to take care of the wages, food and shelter for 318 servants? _____

e. Genesis 14:18-23

According to verses 20 and 21, what did Abram give to Melchizedek, king of Salem?

How would you describe "tithes of all"? _____
_____

TITHE: The Hebrew word for "tithe" is *ma`aser* (pronounced *mah-as-ayr'*) or *ma`asar* (pronounced *mah-as-ar'*), or *ma`asrah* (pronounced *mah-as-raw'*).[2] This literally means tithe, tenth part, payment of a tenth part.

We have discovered that Abraham (Abram) was a man of great wealth and substance. If he gave Melchizedek "tithes of all" — or 10 percent of all he had — that must have been quite a tithe! (Notice this reference to tithing came well before tithing was required under the Mosaic Law and the Levitical priesthood. This is noteworthy because many Christians have discounted tithing as a New Testament doctrine by referring to "tithing" as a principle that was given "under the Law." The theory is that since we are free from "the Law" in Christ, we are free from tithing. But we can see that this type of theology is not grounded in Bible truth. Here Abraham was tithing before the Law concerning tithing had even been given! We will study this subject of tithing further in a later chapter.)

In verses 22 and 23, who did Abram want to be sure received the credit for making him a rich man? _____

f. Genesis 24:22,29-31,35

Again, we see the wealth of Abraham. His servant had been sent with fine gifts to seek a wife for his son, Isaac.

According to verse 22, what did the servant have to give to Rebekah, Isaac's potential wife?_____
_____

Rebekah's brother, Laban, came to see this servant about his inquiry. What did Laban see in verse 30? _____
_____

Based upon what he saw, what did Laban call this servant of Abraham in verse 31?
_____

Laban saw the wealth of Abraham's servant; he had the "blessing of Abraham," and Laban clearly saw it!

In verse 35, how did Abraham's servant describe "the blessing" in Abraham's life? __
_____

g. Genesis 24:1

In looking back over his life, how had the Lord blessed Abraham? _____
_____

The "blessing of Abraham" is ours today through our faith in Jesus Christ! If this servant of God was so incredibly blessed under the Old Covenant, then how much more should we, who qualify for the "blessing of Abraham," be blessed under this "new and better Covenant"?

Let's continue by looking at the "seed of Abraham" and the "blessing of Abraham" that followed his seed.

2. The Prosperity of Isaac:

Isaac was Abraham's son. Let's look at his life.

a. Genesis 25:5,11

In verse 5, Isaac received Abraham's blessing. What was it? _____

In verse 11, whose blessing did Isaac receive? _____

b. Genesis 26:2-4

What did God promise to Isaac, Abraham's seed? _____
_____

c. Genesis 26:12-14,24

Describe the blessings of God that were upon Isaac. _____
_____
_____

Was the "blessing of Abraham" upon him? _____

3. The Prosperity of Jacob:

Jacob was Isaac's son. Let's look at his life.

a. Genesis 27:4,27-30

What did Jacob receive from his father, Isaac? _____
_____

b. Genesis 28:3,4

What did Jacob's father say to him in this blessing? _____
_____
_____

Did you notice that Isaac gave to Jacob the "blessing of Abraham"? _____

c. Genesis 28:20-22

What did Jacob vow to give the Lord of all that the Lord would give to him? _____

_____

Again, we see another Old Covenant believer giving God tithes before the Law of tithing had been initiated.

d. Genesis 32:13-15

   During the years, God had blessed Jacob with much cattle and substance. Jacob, his wives and his family were going to meet his brother Esau, so Jacob wanted to send a gift ahead of them. According to this passage, what type of gift did he send?_____

   _____

   Jacob sent a minimum of 550 animals to his brother! He must have been rich to have taken care of this many animals and their herdsmen!

4. The Prosperity of Joseph:

   Joseph was one of Jacob's beloved sons. Let's look at his life.

   a. Genesis 37:2-5,20

      What does this tell us about Joseph's life? _____

      _____

   b. Genesis 39:1-6,21,23

      Where did Joseph end up? _____

      What does verse 2 tell us about Joseph's relationship with God and about his prosperity? _____

      In verses 3, 21 and 23, what did others notice about Joseph? _____

      _____

      In verses 4-6, we see that God's blessing gave Joseph favor with those around him. What was the result of God's blessing upon him?_____

      _____

      Joseph's life ought to challenge and inspire us. Even in the midst of unpleasant sur-roundings, God's blessings were evident in Joseph's life. How about our lives?

      Do others notice God's blessings and prosperity in our lives? _____

      _____

      Are we receiving favor and promotion because of God's blessing in our lives? _____

      _____

      Do we conduct ourselves with the integrity and diligence we see in Joseph's life?

      _____

Is our employer (or our employees) blessed because of us and because of God's hand of blessing in our lives?_____

_____

c. Genesis 41:37-46

God's blessing in Joseph's life caused him to become the second ruler of the land, directly under Pharaoh.

Describe what happened in verses 37-46. _____

_____

_____

d. Genesis 45:16-23; 47:4-6

Joseph is reunited with his father and brothers. Because of God's blessing upon Joseph, his family is given some tremendous blessings from Pharaoh. Let's look at the abundant wealth and blessing they received.

According to chapter 45, verses 18 and 20, and chapter 47, verse 6, what type of real estate did Pharaoh give them?_____

In chapter 45, verses 21-23, what type of gifts did Joseph give his family?_____

_____

We can clearly see the "blessing of Abraham" on his seed for many generations! Now, let's take a moment to look at the prosperity that was promised to the children of Israel as they walked in light of God's laws.

5. The Prosperity of the Israelites:

Everything about God and His Covenant with man resounds with wealth, riches, abundance — the finest things known to man! When it comes to God's dealings with Israel, God always spoke in terms of blessing, abundance and prosperity! If they would walk in His ways they would be blessed exceedingly! Because He is Almighty God, with whom there is no lack or want, we find that God always speaks to His people in terms that are consistent with His very nature!

For example, we can know much about a person by looking at how he lives and how he speaks. The way he keeps himself, his property and his possessions speak volumes about him. The kind of home he lives in, the kind of clothing he wears, the kind of car he drives will tell you about his personal tastes, his likes and dislikes. The things he talks about and the way he talks about them will tell you quite a bit about him. The same is true about God. We can tell quite a bit about God and His will by observing His "lifestyle." That is, what He prefers, what He talks about and the terms He uses in His Word.

For example, if you think about it, a person's philosophy of life generally determines the type of lifestyle he has adopted and the way he talks about it. The person with a "poverty philosophy" will probably prefer to live, drive, shop and dress in ways that are consistent with that philosophy. It's unlikely that you will find a person who values poverty being comfortable with any type of lavish lifestyle. His conversation will tend to be consistent with his philosophy. He will probably talk about lack, about just making ends meet, about getting by, about living paycheck to paycheck. (If this has described you, don't be condemned! Many of us are guilty of talking this way. But we can renew our minds to God's Word, and we can change what we have been saying!)

In the same way, the person with a "prosperity philosophy" will probably prefer to live, drive, shop and dress in ways that are consistent with that philosophy. It's unlikely that you will find a person who values prosperity being comfortable with anything less. His conversation will tend to be consistent with his philosophy. He will probably talk about abundance and about excess to spend, give, save and invest!

The point is, you can tell much about people's philosophy of life simply by observing the way they live and speak. Again, we can also tell quite a bit about God by looking at how He lives and how He speaks to His people. We can tell much about His personal tastes, His likes and dislikes, by looking at the kind of dwelling place He instructed Moses to make and the way He talked to the Israelites about prosperity. With this thought in mind, let's take a look at God's "lifestyle" and the way He spoke to His people. What type of "philosophy" does God have when it comes to prosperity?

a. Exodus 25:8 through 28:43

   In studying this passage of Scripture that reveals God's plan and instructions for the sanctuary the Israelites were to make for God's presence, take note of the following things:

   What type of precious metal(s) did God require? _____
   _____

   What type of fabrics were to be used? _____
   _____

   What type of precious stones and gems were to be used? _____
   _____

   What types of wood were to be used? _____
   _____

   What types of skins were to be used? _____
   _____

What types of spices and oils were to be used? _____

_____

What types of colors were to be used? _____

_____

Was there anything cheap, inferior, weak, synthetic or recycled about the sanctuary, furnishings or clothing? _____

_____

Did God spare any expense? _____

Understanding that we can tell much about a person by where he lives, in addition to God's holiness, what do God's instructions about His dwelling place tell us about God? _____

   b. Deuteronomy 8:7-18; 11:11-21

These passages summarize what God told the children of Israel about the land into which He was leading them. He was leading them into tremendous prosperity and an ultimate home in quite a "neighborhood!"

What type of land, prosperity and blessings did God promise His people if they would walk in His ways? _____

_____

_____

Let's look at one more evidence of God's will concerning prosperity by looking at the life of David and God's blessing of riches and wealth in and through him.

6. Prosperity in the Life of David:

Once again, we can see God's blessing of prosperity upon one of His servants. In these next passages, God has instructed David to prepare to build Him a house. Although it was David's son Solomon who actually constructed this great house, God gave David the plan for building the house, and David was largely involved in financing its construction. Let's look at the life of David in these passages.

   a. 1 Chronicles 22:5,11-16

In verse 5, how did David describe the house that would be fitting for the Lord?

_____

MAGNIFICAL: The Hebrew word translated "magnifical" is *gadal* (pronounced *gaw-dal*).[3] Its meaning includes to be large, to grow, become great and excellent, promote, praise, magnify.

According to verses 14-16, David prepared for the building of the house of God by giving:

How much gold? _____

How much silver? _____

If David had prepared this much gold in our modern day, by using the current price of gold,[4] we find that his gift of gold alone would be equivalent to the following:

GOLD: Using our conservative figures of 1 "talent" of gold being equivalent to $29,085, we find that 100,000 "talents" of gold equals $29,085,000,000 ($29 billion!)[5]

To convert the value of a "talent" to our modern equivalent, we multiply 125 Troy pounds x 12 Troy ounces to get 1500 Troy ounces per "talent." We then multiply 1500 Troy ounces x $350 (the current price of gold per Troy ounce) to get $525,000 as the modern value of 1 talent of gold.

We find that David's gift of 100,000 talents would be equivalent to $52,500,000,000 ($52.5 billion!) in modern terms!

SILVER: Authorities such as *Smith's Bible Dictionary* and *Dakes Annotated Reference Bible* tell us that a "talent" of silver was equivalent to about 100 Troy pounds and worth about $1,920 conservatively. If we calculate the modern equivalent using the current price of silver, we can figure that 1 "talent" of silver was equal to 100 Troy pounds, or 1200 Troy ounces. Twelve hundred ounces multiplied by the current price of $5.00 an ounce gives us a figure of $6,000 as a modern equivalent for one talent of silver. We see that conservatively David's silver preparation was worth about $1,920,000,000 and possibly $6,000,000,000 ($6 billion) in modern terms!

David had received this primarily through the offerings of the Israelites. What type of house could one build today for over $87 billion?

How much brass and iron? _____

How much timber and stone? _____

How many workers? _____

Is there anything shabby about God's house? _____

How much gold and silver were available? _____

b. 1 Chronicles 29:2-14

According to verses 3-5, what had David personally set aside to give to the house of God? _____

_____

By using our modern-day prices of gold and silver, David's personal offering would be equivalent to the following:

GOLD: 3,000 talents of gold using our conservative figure of $29,085 per talent would equal $87,255,000! If we use our modern equivalent of 1 "talent"of gold equal to $525,000, then David's gift equals $1,575,000,000 ($1,575,000,000!) Either way you look at it David's personal offering was immense to say the least!!

SILVER: 7,000 talents of silver using our conservative figure of $1,920 per talent gives us an equivalency of $13,440,000! Using our modern equivalent of $6,000 per "talent" of silver, we find David's offering of silver to be equal to $42,000,000! ($42 million!)

According to verses 10-13, David blesses and praises God. According to David, who gives riches and honor? _____

Apparently, David knew what he was talking about! God had blessed him and he was a very prosperous man! He was wealthy, and he was a giver! He was an excellent leader and steward over the wealth God's people had contributed to the "building pro-gram." It's obvious that David's heart was in the right place as he gave God glory and praise for His blessings of riches and honor!

It's clear from this chapter, as we have studied passages in both the Old and New Testaments, looking at both the Old and New Covenants, that we can clearly see God's desire for prosperity in the lives of His children. As we looked into the lives of several Old Testament believers, it became evident that God's will for them and their families was abundant prosperity — not just "making ends meet." They were extremely wealthy to the point that those around them took notice!

We have looked at the life of Abraham and at the "blessing of Abraham" that has come on us, who are the "seed of Abraham and heirs according to the promise," as a result of our faith in Jesus Christ. We have seen that one aspect of the "blessing of Abraham" included tremendous wealth! We have also looked at God's blessing of prosperity in the lives of Moses and of the Israelites and in the life of David. We have seen God's "philosophy" for prosperity revealed in part by His instructions for His dwelling place.

It is clear that, under the Old Covenant, God wanted His people to be blessed with prosperity. Therefore, we must conclude that, under our "new and better Covenant," prosperity is indeed God's will for the believer who walks in the light of God's Word!

D. PERSONAL APPLICATION

Can you see that prosperity — abundant wealth — was God's will for the Old Testament saints? Can you see that through Jesus Christ you have become "the seed of Abraham and an heir of the promise"? Do you believe that the "blessing of Abraham" included prosperous living? Are you inspired by the prosperity of Moses and the Israelites, and of King David? Has your vision for obtaining wealth and for giving wealth to the work of God been enlarged? Why not take a moment and pray this prayer from your heart to let the Lord know of your belief in His Word and His will for your life:

Dear Father God, I thank You for revealing Your will for my prosperity from Your Word. I can see Your blessing on Your people, beginning with Abraham and going right on through to the New Testament. I see that the "blessing of Abraham" included wealth and prosperity. I believe that through Jesus Christ I have become the seed of Abraham and an heir of the promise You gave to Him — and that promise does include prosperity, among other things.

Lord, I see that Moses, the children of Israel and King David walked in abundant prosperity as they followed You under the Old Covenant. Some of this is new to my thinking, but I do see it in Your Word, Father, and by faith I believe Your will for me is indeed prosperity.

I ask You, Lord, to continue to give me the knowledge and wisdom I need to walk in Your will and to be a good steward of all the wealth and prosperity You desire for my life. I commit myself to use my life and all of Your blessings in my life for Your glory and for the advancement of Your kingdom. In Jesus' name. Amen.

CHAPTER SIX

"POOR JESUS"

WAS JESUS REALLY POOR?

Was Jesus poor? Did He model the lifestyle of a poor person, and are we to follow His example? Let's answer this question.

WAS JESUS POOR?

As we look at what the Bible reveals to us, you may have to take off your traditional, religious thinking. For many of us, our view of Jesus has been that of a poor baby lying in a manger — so poor, in fact, that His parents couldn't even afford a hotel room the night He was born! We have pictured Him as the Man Who walked the shores of Galilee wearing a robe and sandals. In some ways we have viewed Him as a "holy, but homeless, person." We have pictured His lifestyle somewhat akin to the Jesus Movement of the 1960s, and it would absolutely shatter our traditional thinking to see Jesus in the '90s, wearing a suit and tie!

What was Jesus' standard of living when He walked on earth? If we compare His heavenly dwelling and His eternal existence with the Father to His life on earth, it would be considered poor by comparison! However, when equating His lifestyle on earth with the lifestyle of that day, was Jesus really poor? Did He by virtue of His own lifestyle absolutely repudiate the prosperity message? These are valid questions, and we want to answer them.

For many New Testament believers, this is a critical issue. If we are to be like our Master, we must know what He was like, particularly in this area of prosperous living. So let's take a look at numerous Scriptures regarding this subject.

A. JESUS WAS PROSPEROUS AS A YOUNG CHILD

Matthew 2:1-11

According to verses 1 and 2, who came looking for the "King of the Jews"? _____

_____

Does the Bible tell us how many wise men there were? _____

Tradition has told us there were 3 wise men, but the Bible doesn't say specifically that there were only three, there could have been more.

According to verse 11, where did these wise men find Jesus? _____
_____

Scholars tell us that this "house" was not the manger in which Jesus was born but rather where He lived in Nazareth after He was taken to Jerusalem to be presented to the Lord. (Luke 2:22; Lev. 12:2-6.)

Does verse 11 describe Jesus as a "baby" or a "young child"? _____
_____

Again, scholars tell us Jesus was probably about two years old at the time the wise men visited Him.

What did the wise men present to Jesus? _____
_____

When Jesus was a young child, He was presented with gold (certainly a form of currency), frankincense and myrrh. This was quite a substantial gift. Jesus began His life with prosperity!

B. JESUS HAD A HOME

The traditional view about Jesus' home has been that He didn't have one. This thought is based upon the statement found in Matthew 8:20, **And Jesus saith unto him, The foxes have holes, and the birds of the air have nests; but the Son of man hath not where to lay his head.** With this in mind, many have viewed Jesus as an original, homeless person. Actually, the Bible tells us that Jesus had a place to live.

John 1:38,39

According to verse 38, what did Jesus' followers want to know? _____
_____

In verse 39, what did they see? _____

Although this passage does not tell us much about Jesus' home, it is clear that He had a place to live. His followers were able to see it and to spend the day with Him there.

C. JESUS RECEIVED THE PROSPERITY OF OTHERS

John 12:1-8

According to verse 3, what did Mary do with the "ointment of spikenard"? _____
_____

In verse 3, how much spikenard was used? _____

What does verse 3 tell us about the cost of this ointment?_____
_____

Judas describes in verse 5 how much this ointment could have been sold for. What does this
tell us about the value of the ointment?_____
_____

A PENCE: A pence was equal to about 17 cents, or a day's wage; 300 pence was equivalent
to about $51, or about a year's worth (300 days) of wages.[1]

This was expensive ointment! When was the last time you spent a year's wages on perfume?
Let's take this a little farther and convert these figures into modern equivalents. To be conservative, let's say the average American worker earns $5 per hour and works 40 hours per
week. This would total $10,400 annually before taxes. Can you imagine owning a bottle of
perfume worth nearly $10,000?

What would you think about a person who owned a bottle of perfume that expensive? _____
_____

Did it bother Jesus that Mary had such an expensive jar of ointment? _____
_____

Did He rebuke Mary for "wasting" this expensive ointment?_____

Who rebuked her for "wasting" the ointment? _____

If Jesus were appalled at Mary's wealth, do you think He would have allowed her to anoint
Him with the ointment? _____

D. JESUS RODE THE TRANSPORTATION OF A PROSPEROUS MAN

1. Mark 11:1-7

    According to verse 2, what type of animal did Jesus commission His disciples to obtain?
    _____

2. Judges 10:4; 12:14

What did the sons of the judges of Israel ride on? _____

Riding the colt was a sign of distinction. The rulers of the cities were prominent in the land, and riding a colt was appropriate for their position.

E. JESUS WORE THE CLOTHING OF A PROSPEROUS PERSON

John 19:23,24

What did the soldiers take of Jesus' clothing? _____

How is His coat described? _____

COAT: This is from the Greek word *chiton* (pronounced *khee-tone'*), which means a tunic or a shirt.[2] We see here that Jesus had on several garments — an undergarment or "coat" which the soldiers cast lots for, and outer garments which the soldiers divided among them. From the way the soldiers treated Jesus' coat, there evidently had to be some value to it, for what did the soldiers do with it?_____

F. JESUS HAD FINANCIAL PARTNERS AND A TREASURER FOR HIS MINISTRY

1. Luke 8:1-3

Who were the women that ministered to Jesus?_____
_____

What did they minister to Him? _____

"Their substance" is a reference to Jesus' ministry support, which included money as well as material things. We know Jesus never lacked for anything. In addition to the support He received from these women, we know He operated in the realm of the miraculous!

2. John 12:4-6; 13:29

According to these verses, what was Judas' responsibility in Jesus' ministry?_____
_____

In John 12:6, what is Judas called? _____

What does a thief do? _____

There must have been enough money in Jesus' ministry to require one of His disciples to act as treasurer. This responsibility was given to Judas. In addition, the need for a treasurer implies that there must have been something in the bag worth stealing! Part of the finances of Jesus' ministry must have been the "substance" the women had ministered to Him.

According to John 13:29, there must have been a considerable amount of money in the bag because of what the disciples thought Jesus had said to Judas. What did they think He said? _____
_____

If the disciples thought Judas had enough money in the bag to buy supplies for the feast, there had to be quite a sum of money, because that feast lasted seven days!

On another occasion, in Mark 6:34-44, we see Jesus ministering to 5,000 men, plus women and children. In verse 37, as it grew late in the day, He told His disciples to give the multitude something to eat. They replied, **Shall we go and buy two hundred pennyworth of bread, and give them to eat?** Jesus' response was to perform a miracle, which we have come to know as the miracle of the loaves and fishes. However, there is an important point we don't want to overlook: apparently, the disciples had some money — 200 pennyworth! One penny, or denarius as it was also known, was worth 15 to 17 cents, so 200 pennyworth was the equivalent of $30 to $34. Though this doesn't seem like much in our current day, we see from what Jesus said at that time in Matthew 20:2 that a day's wages were equivalent to one penny, or a denarius. Therefore, 200 pennyworth would be equivalent to 200 days' wages. In other words, in their liquid "savings account," they had over a half-year's wages on hand.[3] How many of us have six months' worth of wages in our liquid savings account?

G. JESUS ASSOCIATED WITH PROSPEROUS PEOPLE

1. Luke 5:27-32

   What did Jesus say to Levi (Matthew), the tax collector? _____
   _____

   What did Levi do in verse 28? _____

   What type of feast did Levi have for Jesus? _____

   Where was this feast held? _____

   How many people attended? _____

Levi must have had quite a large house to accommodate this great feast. He invited a great company of his "sinner" friends and introduced them to Jesus. But Jesus neither rebuked Levi for his wealth, nor told him he would have to sell it all to give to the poor.

As a matter of fact, we see in verses 30-32 that the scribes and Pharisees murmured about Jesus hanging out with publicans and sinners while enjoying food and drink in their presence. No doubt this was a reference to the party at Levi's house. What was Jesus' response? _____

_____

_____

2. Luke 19:1-8

How does verse 2 describe Zacchaeus? _____

_____

What did Jesus want to do with Zacchaeus? _____

How did Zacchaeus respond after he had spent time with Jesus? _____

_____

H. JESUS PRACTICED WHAT HE PREACHED

1. Matthew 6:33

According to this verse, what did Jesus tell others to do? _____

_____

Do you think Jesus sought first the kingdom of God and His righteousness? _____

_____

If He did obey this verse, were all things added unto Him? _____

2. Luke 6:38

What did Jesus tell His followers to do? _____

If they obeyed this verse, what would result? _____

_____

Was Jesus a giver? _____

If He obeyed this verse, do you think men gave into His bosom? _____

_____

I. JESUS BECAME POOR FOR OUR PROSPERITY

This may sound like a contradiction of what we have been studying concerning the life of Jesus, but let's take a closer look at this.

The Bible tells us about the substitutionary work of Christ on our behalf. For example, we see Jesus as our substitute in the area of sin, according to 2 Corinthians 5:21: **For he hath made him to be sin for us, who knew no sin; that we might be made the righteousness of God in him.** In other words, Jesus Who knew no sin became our substitute on the cross and took sin on our behalf so that we could be made the righteousness of God in Him. Because of Jesus' substitutionary work, God sees us as righteous now!

In the same way, we see Jesus as our substitute in the area of sickness and disease, according to Matthew 8:17: **That it might be fulfilled which was spoken by Esaias** (Isaiah) **the prophet, saying, Himself took our infirmities, and bare our sicknesses.** In other words, Jesus Who knew no sickness or infirmity became our substitute on the cross and took infirmities and sicknesses on our behalf so that we could be healed and healthy in Him. Because of Jesus' substitutionary work, God sees us as healthy and whole right now!

In the same way, Jesus was our substitute in the area of poverty and lack, according to 2 Corinthians 8:9: **For ye know the grace of our Lord Jesus Christ, that, though he was rich, yet for your sakes he became poor, that ye through his poverty might be rich.** In other words, Jesus Who knew no poverty became our substitute on the cross where He took poverty on our behalf so that we could be prosperous. Because of Jesus' substitutionary work, God sees us as prosperous right now!

Let's take a moment to look at some of these important Scriptures.

1. 2 Corinthians 8:9

    Before Jesus came to earth, how is He described? _____
    _____

    Compared to His heavenly life, how is His earthly life described? _____
    _____

    In a sense, Jesus' earthly life was poor when compared to what He was accustomed to in heaven. However, as we have seen, His earthly life was not a life of poverty.

    On the cross Jesus became poor that we might be rich. He took upon Himself our sin, our sickness, our poverty so that we might be redeemed from eternal death and separation from God, from sickness and disease, from poverty.

    Through Christ's poverty, what do we have? _____

2. Isaiah 53:5

   In this great redemptive chapter, we see God's desire for His children to be blessed in spirit and soul and body, and we see a glimpse of God's desire for His children to prosper!

   In verse 5, Jesus was chastised for what?_____

   The Hebrew word translated "peace" in this verse is translated "prosperity" other places in the Bible. We could read this phrase as, "...the chastisement of our *prosperity* was upon him." Actually, this makes redemptive sense. We know from the whole of Scripture that Jesus redeemed us from sin, from sickness and from poverty. When we read it this way, it actually confirms our redemption in all three of these areas!

Have your traditional views been challenged a bit in this chapter? Can you see from Scripture that Jesus was not the poor man in a robe and sandals that we have often thought Him to be? Jesus was prosperous in His earth walk; He became poor on the cross so that through His poverty we might be rich.

J. PERSONAL APPLICATION

JESUS' MINISTRY

It may take some time to renew your mind to this material, because for years the Christian church at large has viewed Jesus as poor. We have seen Him leading a simple life with the barest of necessities to get along. So take a moment to remove those traditional views and see Jesus' ministry in the light of what is written in the Word. Think about these questions...

1. In addition to the supernatural, miraculous supply we see in Jesus' ministry (changing water into wine, the coin in the fish's mouth, the breaking of the loaves and fishes, etc.) what type of ministry did He lead on a daily basis? We have seen from previous Scriptures in our study that Jesus had financial supporters and partners. We have also seen that Jesus had a treasurer (Judas — a thief!) who kept track of their finances. So, if the ministry income Jesus had coming in truly was only "nickels and dimes" it probably would not have been necessary to assign someone to the position of treasurer.

2. How many people were on Jesus' "staff?" We know there were at least the 12 disciples, plus the wives and children of those disciples who were married. We don't know to what degree Jesus supported his mother and/or any of his brothers and sisters, but we do know that Jesus obeyed the Word to honor his mother and father. We do not hear much about Joseph in the life of Jesus after he was 12 years old. Many scholars believe that Joseph may have died while Jesus was a young man. So it is possible that Jesus took care of His mother's financial needs as well.

3. Do you believe that Jesus was a fair employer? If Jesus told twelve people to quit their jobs to follow Him, do you think that Jesus would allow them and their families to go hungry because of their change of occupation in seeking first the kingdom of God? Do you think once these twelve made the decision to leave everything to follow Jesus that they had to work a second job "moonlighting" to support themselves or their families? Absolutely not! If you think about it, Jesus must have had enough resources to financially support twelve men and their families. This includes their lodging/housing, meals, travel expenses, and even taxes! If you were to add twelve people to your staff or ministry, what kind of resources would it take to employ such a team of people? Jesus must have been walking in a large degree of faith for prosperous living to have supported such a ministry staff.

These thoughts may be new to you, but they are scriptural and worth meditating upon. Remember, we are renewing our minds to the Word of God, the truth, and we are shedding the "traditions of men" which make the Word of God of no effect!

CHAPTER SEVEN

"GOD'S ECONOMY"
WHAT SHOULD WE EXPECT FROM GOD?

When it comes to this area of prosperous living, what should we expect God to do for us? Is it fair to pray for prosperity, then expect God to send a Saint Bernard with a barrel of money around its neck in answer to our plea? Is it scriptural to claim a certain amount of money, then lounge around waiting for the checks to magically appear in our mailbox on a daily basis?

What should we expect from God in this area of prosperity? When it comes to the things of God, have you ever wondered whose court the ball is in? In other words, when we are desiring something from God, how do we know if the ball is in our court and we must make a move, or if the ball is in God's court and by faith we must wait on Him?

God has laid down certain laws and principles in this area of prosperous living, and if we cooperate with them, we can expect them to work. Being involved in God's economy is different than just being involved in the world's economy. In fact, in some areas God's laws are contrary to popular, secular economic thought. We want to study the idea of honoring God with our wealth; of giving to the Lord in tithes, offerings and alms; and of acting by the law of sowing and reaping. Let's take a look at this subject by examining the Scriptures.

A. GOD BLESSES THOSE WHO TITHE TO HIS CHURCH

There are many questions and arguments about the issue of tithing. • Is tithing a command for New Testament Christians? • Is tithing just an Old Testament principle for those under the Law? • From which amount of the income is a person supposed to tithe — the net or the gross? • Can a person tithe more than 10 percent, or less than 10 percent? • Where should a person give his tithes: to the local church or other evangelistic ministries?

Let's take away our preconceived ideas about tithing, and let's look at what the Bible says about it.

1. What is the "tithe?"

   TITHE: Again, the Hebrew word for "tithe" is *ma`aser* (pronounced *mah-as-ayr'*), or *ma`asar* (pronounced *mah-as-ar'*) or *ma`asrah* (pronounced *mah-as-raw'*).[1] It literally means the tenth part or the payment of a tenth part.

In other words, the tithe technically represents 10 percent of a person's income or increase.

2. Who is supposed to tithe?

Is tithing an Old Testament principle that New Testament Christians are required to abide by? Is tithing a New Testament principle? Is tithing for the Christian optional?

We are going to look at what the Bible says about who is supposed to tithe. As we explore God's Word on this subject, we will find that tithing existed *before* the Law, *under* the Law and *after* the Law was fulfilled in Jesus Christ. So let's consider each of these areas.

Tithing *Under* the Law

Let's look at a more thorough definition of tithing as defined *under* the Law. The law of the tithe was instituted under Moses and the Levitical priesthood. *Under* the Law, God's people were expected to tithe! It was not optional!

a. Leviticus 27:30-32

According to the commandment of the Lord, what were the Israelites supposed to tithe to the Lord? _____

_____

In Old Testament times, Israel's industry was primarily agricultural. God expected His people to give Him 10 percent of all their increase, whether it be land or crops or livestock. Ten percent of their livelihood belonged to God. That was the Law!

In verse 31, if a person under the Law didn't pay his tithes, how much of a "penalty" was he to pay in addition to the tithe? _____

In other words, under the Law, if a person didn't pay his tithes, he was required as a penalty to pay an additional 20 percent!

b. Exodus 23:19; Deuteronomy 14:22,23; 26:2

What were God's people supposed to tithe to the Lord? _____

_____

c. Malachi 3:8-12

Who was God talking to in this passage? _____

What were they to bring to God's storehouse? _____

How had they robbed God? _____

Under the Law, the Israelites were required to tithe; if they did not, God considered it robbery! To rob someone by definition presupposes that it was theirs to begin with. One hundred percent of our income belongs to God, and it was considered robbery when God's people did not give Him 10 percent of their income.

d. Luke 11:42

Jesus rebuked the religious leaders of His day because they were intent on keeping the letter of the Law, but overlooked the weightier matter of love. These Pharisees were tithing as those *under* the Law. Was Jesus impressed with their obligatory duty? _____

_____

Jesus was not impressed, and He told them so. However, if Jesus had come to do away with tithing, wouldn't this have been a good time for Him to announce that He had come to fulfill the Law and that tithing was not going to be a New Testament principle?

_____

Instead of abolishing the tithe, what did Jesus tell these Pharisees about their duty to tithe? Did He tell them to quit tithing or to continue tithing? _____

_____

We can see that, *under* the Law, the tithe represented 10 percent of a person's income, the first fruits of all his or her increase. When this is put into perspective, we can see what God was saying to His people. As Scripture says, **The earth is the Lord's, and the fulness thereof** (Ps. 24:1). So technically 100 percent of His people's income and the first fruits of their increase really belonged to God. But God was kind enough to allow them to keep 90 percent of their income to use for living expenses and for the comforts of life, while requiring that only 10 percent be given back to Him. In light of this, tithing 10 percent of their income to God's work was the *least* they could do! Tithing was the bare minimum!

Most believers accept the fact that tithing was a requirement for those under the Law, but what about the requirement to tithe *before* or *after* the Law?

Tithing *Before* the Law

Did people tithe before the Law was ever instituted? The answer is yes!

The first reference to tithes in Scripture is found in Genesis 14:20,21. In this instance, Abram (Abraham) tithed years *before* the Law was ever instituted! Abram tithed out of a heart that was willing to give — not under compulsion or the Law. This is the account where Abram gave tithes of all he had to Melchizedek, king of Salem. It is clear from reading verse 21 that Abram's tithe included 10 percent of his wealth in material goods.

a. Genesis 14:18-21

What did Abram give to Melchizedek? _____

_____

We see another reference to tithing in Genesis 28:20-22, where Jacob vowed to give the Lord a tenth of all the Lord gave to him. Jacob was not obligated to give the Lord a tenth according to the Law, because the Law didn't exist at that time. Jacob gave his tithe to the Lord out of a heart of gratitude — not compulsion.

b. Genesis 28:20-22

What did Jacob vow to give to the Lord? _____

_____

So we can clearly see that God's people were tithers *before* it was required by Law! They tithed ten percent of all they had because they loved God and they must have known something about God's economic laws. If you will review, you will find that Abram (Abraham) and Jacob were some of the wealthiest persons in the Bible. Tithing certainly didn't hurt their financial status! Tithing *before* the Law was defined as one-tenth of a person's wealth, or we could say that ten percent of all a person had was his tithe.

Tithing *After* the Law

a. Luke 16:16

When did the principles governing the obligation to obey the Law and the Old Testament prophets end? _____

_____

When did the principles governing obedience to the kingdom of God begin? _____

_____

b. Luke 11:42

What did Jesus say in this verse about tithing under the kingdom of God *after* the Law?

_____

_____

c. Hebrews 7:1-8

This passage refers to the account of Abraham (Abram) giving tithes to King Melchizedek *before* the Law. It is also a reference to and a type of Christian believers giving tithes *after* the Law to our King, Jesus Christ. As Abraham gave tithes *before* the Law to the high priest, Melchizedek, we (the seed of Abraham) give tithes *after* the Law to our High Priest, Jesus Christ. Both Abraham and New Testament believers give tithes as an act of worship and love for God — not under compulsion as a duty of the Law!

According to verse 8, when we give our tithes, who receives them here on earth?

_____

According to verse 8, when we give our tithes, who receives them in heaven? _____

_____

In other words, in the natural realm when we bring our tithes to our local church, it is mortal men and women on earth (that is, the ushers and pastors, etc. in the Church) who receive them. In the spiritual realm, it is Jesus Christ Himself Who receives our tithes. It would do us well to keep this picture in mind as we bring our tithes to our local church each week. Although we place our envelope in an offering basket here on earth, in heaven Jesus Christ Himself is receiving our tithes as an act of our love and worship.

NOTE: Some have asked if we should tithe off the gross income or the net. Perhaps this is a matter of personal conscience. There are people who by faith are tithing off their gross, while others by faith are tithing off their net. Whatever you choose to do, do it by faith, trusting in God's promises to the tither. Here is food for thought: some believers are tithing by faith on the amount of money they desire to earn for a given year. For example, let's say a person earns $50,000 per year but is believing God for increase so that he can earn $60,000 per year. Instead of tithing off the $50,000, which would equal a yearly tithe of $5,000, by faith he decides to tithe off the $60,000 he is expecting to earn by giving $6,000. He is tithing off the increased amount for which he is believing God to receive.

3. Where are we supposed to tithe?

   a. Deuteronomy 12:11; 14:23

   Where were the Israelites to bring their tithe? _____

   _____

   A place which the Lord your God shall choose to cause his name to dwell there (v. 11) is referring to the tabernacle of Moses. God's people were to bring their tithes to the house of God.

   b. Malachi 3:10

   Where did God tell His people to bring their tithes, or 10 percent of their income?

   _____

How much of the tithe (10 percent) were they supposed to bring to the storehouse?

_____

Notice *all* the tithe was supposed to go to the storehouse. In other words, we are to bring the entire 10 percent to the storehouse. It is not scriptural to subdivide our tithe and give it to various or multiple ministries. We may give offerings to various ministries, over and above our tithe, but the tithe itself belongs in its entirety to the storehouse.

In your own words, where would you define the storehouse to be? _____

_____

To what is the storehouse referring? Is this a reference to the local church? Is it possible to give tithes to a TV ministry, an itinerant teaching or preaching ministry, a missions outreach or a program that reaches the poor?

Although we are thoroughly supportive of any and all ministries God raises up to preach the Gospel of Jesus Christ, and we heartily advocate giving offerings to any and all of these types of ministries, we believe the Scriptures teach us to bring our tithes — ten percent of our income — to the local church which we attend. Of course, this implies that we attend a local church. (If you aren't committed to regularly attending a local church, we encourage you to spend some time with God, studying His Word on this matter. It is God's plan to build strong local churches where His Word, His presence and the ministry of the Holy Spirit are in full manifestation. You need to be a part of what God is doing on the earth in and through His local church!)

The storehouse is a reference to the place of treasure, or treasury. Where do you get your spiritual treasures? Most people agree that this is a reference to the local church. The local church you attend is your spiritual storehouse. It is there that God has gifted the pastor and the church staff to minister to your needs. It is there that you receive the ministry of the Word, which feeds you spiritually, and you are supported in prayer when faced with the needs of life. At your local church, you find a family who helps to meet your natural needs in times of distress and trouble. They visit you in the hospital. They receive your late-night phone calls. They dedicate your babies, marry your children and perform funerals for your loved ones. The local church storehouse is indeed a rich spiritual treasury. Every Christian should be convinced and committed to bringing all their tithes into their storehouse on a regular basis. It is the faithful and regular giving of tithers that will keep local church storehouses strong all around the world! (We believe in the value of itinerant ministry, missions work, TV and radio ministry, etc. and these should be supported with offerings over and above our tithe.)

How are you supposed to get all your tithes to the storehouse?

_____Mail your tithe?   _____Fax your tithe?

_____Charge your tithe?   _____Bring your tithe?

The word *bring* implies that we are to personally bring our tithe to the storehouse, the local church, which we attend on a regular basis. Of course, there may be a special occasion on which you are unable to attend physically, and may need to mail it.

Why were the tithes supposed to be brought to the storehouse? _____
_____

There can't be "meat" in God's house (the local church) unless tithes are brought to the storehouse (the local church).

We see a twofold application to the words, "meat in My house".

First, many times in Scripture, we see "meat" as a reference to the mature things of God's Word, or "revelation knowledge." Did you know that as you tithe you can expect God to give you "meat?" That means revelation knowledge and understanding of the mature things of God's Word!

Second, whether we like it or not, it takes finances to give a church "meat" — that is, the provisions it needs to pioneer, build, grow, staff and expand a church and its outreach efforts locally and around the world. The tithe was and is God's plan for financing His Church and the outreach of His Gospel around the world.

c. Haggai 1:2-11

This is the story of God's people who were more concerned about their own houses than about the house of God. In other words, they were more interested in their lives and homes than in the things of God and His house. What did the Lord tell them to do in verses 5 and 7?_____
_____

Because of their disobedience and their wrong priorities, they were obviously not walking in the blessings attached to the tither. According to verses 6 and 9-11, what was happening in the financial and material areas of their lives?_____
_____

If they wanted to walk in God's blessings, what were they to do, according to verse 8?
_____

Can you see any parallels in this story with your own life?_____
_____

If so, are you ready to make the necessary changes and to commit to being a regular tither to your local church? _____

4. What are the benefits of tithing?

On one hand, the greatest benefit of tithing is that it gives the New Testament Christian a chance to demonstrate in a tangible way his or her worship and love for God with more than just lip service. On the other hand, God in His generosity has attached blessings to the tithe. Let's take a few moments to look at the blessings that are promised to those who tithe.

Malachi 3:8-12

We see the clearest picture of God's blessings for those who tithe in this passage from the book of Malachi.

a. Let's look at the bad news first. In what areas did God say His people had robbed Him?_____
_____

Notice in verse 8 He said, **In tithes *and* offerings**. We will discuss the subject of offerings in the next section, but for now we will focus on the tithe.

What was the result of robbing God in this area of tithes and offerings? _____
_____

What do you think it means to be "cursed with a curse"? _____
_____

A curse is bad enough — but to be cursed with a curse — that's a curse multiplied!

For more details on the curses, look at Deuteronomy 28:15-68.

b. God actually exhorts us to prove Him in this area of tithing.

What four things does He promise will happen if we tithe?

1. _____

2. _____

3. _____

4. _____

(1) God promises to "open the windows of heaven" for those of us who tithe. Genesis 7:11 and 8:2 give us a picture of what it means for the "windows of heaven" to be opened. In the days of Noah, God opened the windows of heaven and allowed rain to flood the earth. So when God opens His windows, things flood!

I don't believe God intended for us to place our tithe in the offering basket, then just walk outside and begin to gaze up, waiting for dollar bills to come floating down from the windows of heaven. But I do believe we are to expect the windows of heaven to be opened for us.

A good minister friend of mine often uses the phrase, "windows of opportunity," as a definition for "windows of heaven." His idea is that God allows us, as tithers, to see through a "window" that perhaps we had not seen before, and He allows us to have the knowledge of witty ideas or inventions (Prov. 8:12) as we see through that window. Opportunities that perhaps we had been blinded to are now opened up to us as tithers. When you consistently place your tithe in the offering basket at your local church, you should begin to expect the windows of heaven and opportunity to open up to you. Expect God to give you new ideas, new opportunities, and even inventions, that will be a blessing to you and to those around you!

(2) God promises to pour you out a blessing that there shall not be room enough to receive. That sounds like what Jesus said in Luke 6:38: **Give, and it shall be given unto you; good measure, pressed down, and shaken together, and running over, shall men give into your bosom.** Blessings are running over! As a tither, you should begin to expect God's blessings on *every* hand!

(3) God said He would rebuke the devourer for your sake! That means Satan cannot destroy that which produces income for the tither. In addition, it sounds like Satan cannot destroy that which your income has purchased. Have you ever noticed that, for some reason, those who tithe seem to have cars, tires, appliances, clothing and other material things that don't seem to break down as often and seem to last longer? God rebukes the devourer for the sake of the tither! That sounds like what God did for the Israelites in the wilderness: their clothes and shoes didn't wear out for forty years! (Deut. 29:5; Neh. 9:21.)

(4) The fourth blessing is **...all nations shall call you blessed: for ye shall be a delightsome land** (Mal. 3:12). I believe God wants others to see His blessings in our lives! When God blesses us with prosperity, others will see it. Prosperity preaches a wonderful message about the goodness of God. As we share with others the blessings of God in our lives — our abundance of food, our homes, our material goods and furnishings — this prosperity preaches a sermon that people in the world can understand!

Many times, the world around us doesn't see us in our prayer closets. They don't see us attending church two or three times each week. They don't see us reading our Bibles or praising the Lord or wearing a "halo." But they do see our lifestyle, and one thing the world can recognize is prosperity!

For years, when I knew virtually nothing about God's will to prosper me, I was one of those sincere Christians who loved God with all my heart as I drove around in my rusted "beater" car with a "Jesus Is Lord" sticker plastered on its bumper. In looking back, I wonder what kind of a witness that really was? One thing is for sure: when I was driving around in that car and praising the Lord, the heathen weren't saying, "Wow, God has really blessed her!" Now don't get me wrong — I'm not saying you have to drive a brand-new import to "prove" God's blessing in your life. Even though the "nations" weren't exactly calling me blessed in my rusty old car, God still loved me and I loved Him — and I *was* blessed! However, there is a truth that we need to look at along these lines: when we are blessed with prosperity, we have an expanded opportunity to be a blessing to others and to let our light shine before men in a language they will understand!

It is clear that God blesses those who tithe to His Church. Tithing — *after* the Law, under the New Covenant — is the same as it was *before* the Law, under the Old Covenant. As Christians, we, like Abraham, tithe because we want to demonstrate our love and worship to God. We do so cheerfully, not under compulsion. As a result, we are qualified to receive the blessings attached to the tithe. Tithing is one of the essentials of operating in God's economy. Giving ten percent of our income to God is the minimum amount every Christian ought to be investing back into God's kingdom. In connection with tithing, the Bible talks about honoring God with our wealth. Let's look at this subject now.

B. GOD BLESSES THOSE WHO HONOR HIM WITH THEIR WEALTH

1. Proverbs 3:9,10 — Honoring God:

   What are we to honor the Lord with? _____
   _____

   What type of "substance" do you have? _____
   _____

   How would you define the "first fruits of all thine increase"? _____
   _____

   Are you honoring the Lord with your substance and with the first fruits of all your increase? How could you do better in this area? _____
   _____

   According to verse 10, what is the result of honoring God with our wealth?_____
   _____

Once we have cooperated with God's law of honoring Him with our wealth, it is God's responsibility to fill our barns with plenty!

2. Luke 12:15-21 — Dishonoring God:

This is the story of a man who did not honor God with his wealth. What does verse 21 tell us about this man and his wealth? _____

_____

What happened to this man's barns? _____

In talking about honoring the Lord with our wealth, we want to take a look at two types of people we are to honor with our finances: our natural parents and our spiritual parents (elders).

3. Honoring Earthly Parents:

a. Ephesians 6:1-3

What are we commanded to do toward our parents? _____

_____

In your own words, what are some ways a person would honor his parents? _____

_____

b. Mark 7:9-13

Jesus rebuked His followers because they weren't honoring their fathers and mothers as God had commanded. It's interesting to note that in honoring parents, Jesus is clearly making a reference to honoring them by taking care of them financially.

What is Jesus talking about in verse 11? _____

_____

The Pharisees and scribes had taught the people that if a son or daughter told his or her parents, "It is Corban" (which in modern language means, "Sorry, Mom and Dad, I can't help you out financially because I'm giving all my money to God"), then those children would be free from their duty to honor their parents in a financial way. Jesus rebuked this type of thinking, saying that they had made the Word of God of no effect by their traditions! In other words, Jesus implied that, as sons and daughters, we do have an obligation to honor our parents by assisting them financially. (We see the Holy Spirit inspiring the apostle Paul to write the same thing about children and their widowed parents in 1 Timothy 5:4,16.)

In other words, it is pleasing to God when we honor our parents by blessing them financially. Hopefully, you are as challenged as I am by these Scriptures to do more for your parents!

4.   Honoring Spiritual Parents:

   a.   1 Timothy 5:17,18

   What did the Lord say should be given to the elders, those who have spiritual over-sight and who teach the Word and doctrine? _____

   _____

   According to verse 18, to what is God comparing the elder? _____

   _____

   In other words, an elder is just like an ox which must be compensated well for the work it is doing under the yoke, having the freedom to eat kernels of corn as it works the field. So too, those who are spiritual leaders under Jesus' yoke must be taken care of; they are worthy of their reward.

   Very often when we think of elders, we just think of our pastor, and that is well and good, but you may need to expand your personal definition of elder for the purposes of honor.

   In your life, who have been your spiritual parents? (In other words, who led you to Jesus Christ and helped to get you established in the foundations of your faith?) _____

   _____

   _____

   Who has been instrumental in teaching you the Word and establishing you in good doctrine? Your pastor? A particular minister's books, tapes, videos or broadcasts? A brother or sister in Christ? _____

   Have you ever honored in a financial way those who are your spiritual parents, who have taught you the Word and doctrine? _____

   b.   1 Corinthians 9:7-11

   In light of this entire passage, what does Paul mean by "sowing spiritual things" and "reaping carnal things"? _____

   _____

   c.   Galatians 6:6

   What is he who is taught the Word exhorted to do for him who teaches the Word? __

   _____

This is a reference to the material/financial support of the teacher.

Hopefully, you are challenged, as I am, to consider honoring in some type of financial or material way, those individuals who have played a vital role in your spiritual growth. What these people have put into our lives cannot be measured in dollars and cents: so as God increases us financially, we can certainly do our best to bless and honor them financially.

We can see, then, that we are to honor the Lord with all that we have! Would you say that your overall lifestyle is one of honoring the Lord and honoring your natural as well as your spiritual parents with your wealth and material possessions?

Let's look now at more practical ways we can cooperate with God's economic laws.

C. GOD BLESSES THOSE WHO GIVE OFFERINGS TO HIS WORKS

1. Malachi 3:8

    In addition to tithes, what else did God say we should give to Him? _____
    _____

    Offerings are what we give to God and His work over and above the tithe, our 10 percent. The first 10 percent belongs to God, and tithing is our way of cheerfully and worshipfully giving it back to God. He allows us to use the other 90 percent of our income for living our lives and for being a blessing to others. When we give any portion of the 90 percent to the Lord, His work or other ministries, we are giving an offering of our own free will to the Lord.

    In the Old Testament, in addition to abiding by the law of the tithe, God's people brought offerings in abundance to the house of God. And God never let His people down either; He made sure they were abundantly taken care of as they walked in the light of His commandments.

2. Exodus 25:1-7; 35:4-9,20-29; 36:3-7

    What did the Lord want the Israelites to do? _____
    _____

    What type of offerings were they to bring?_____
    _____

    According to chapter 25, verse 2, and chapter 35, verses 5, 21, 22, 26 and 29, describe the heart condition of those who gave offerings to the Lord._____
    _____
    _____

Were they giving out of duty, compulsion or guilt?_____

Would you define their offerings as "meager" or "abundant?" _____

_____

_____

According to chapter 36, verses 5-7, what was the result of their offerings? _____

_____

3. Proverbs 11:24,25

What will he who gives to others have? _____

What will he who is stingy have? _____

What is promised to the liberal soul, the person who is a generous giver? _____

_____

_____

What will happen to the person who waters (gives) to others? _____

_____

_____

_____

4. Mark 12:41-44; Luke 21:1-4

What was Jesus watching? _____

What did Jesus think about the rich man's offering? _____

_____

What did Jesus think about the poor widow's offering? _____

_____

5. John 6:5-13

This is the story of a little boy who gave an offering to Jesus. It shows that Jesus can do miraculous things with our offerings!

According to verse 9, what did the little lad have to offer to Jesus? _____

_____

Obviously, the little boy gave these things to Jesus. What did Jesus do with that offering?

_____

_____

How many people (including the men and an estimated number of women and children) did Jesus feed to the full with the five loaves and two small fishes? _____
_____

According to verses 12 and 13, what remained of the loaves and fishes? _____
_____

God can do miracles when we give Him offerings!

6. Luke 6:38

We see a Bible principle here; what are we to do to others? _____
_____
_____

According to verses 31-37, what type of things are we to give to others? _____
_____
_____

Do you see the giving of money or material possessions in any of these verses? If so, which one(s)? _____
_____

What will be the result if we give to others? _____
_____

In what measure or quantity will what we give be returned to us? _____
_____

Who will give to us? _____

If people aren't giving unto you, good measure, pressed down and running over, maybe you need to check up on yourself, on your giving and on the measure you give.

Perhaps you should pray about it and consider those to whom you should give offerings. There are many valid and fruitful ministers/ministries, missionaries, outreach and missions organizations, as well as other projects of the Gospel that would be glad to receive your offerings of support as they work for God. You might want to consider becoming a monthly partner with a particular ministry (or ministries), or maybe supporting a missionary on a monthly basis. You might want to give offerings to a particular need, such as a building fund or missions outreach in your church. You may want to designate a certain amount of money to give in offerings each month, then seek the Lord about where and when and to whom to give your offerings.

In talking about giving offerings, we are describing what the Bible calls the principle of sowing and reaping. Let's look at several other passages that describe in greater detail this law of sowing and reaping.

D. GOD BLESSES THOSE WHO OPERATE IN THE LAWS OF SOWING AND REAPING

The law of sowing and reaping (sometimes called the law of seedtime and harvest or the principle of investment and increase) is found throughout the Word of God.

1. Genesis 8:22

   What did God say would not cease as long as the earth remains? _____
   _____

   We see evidence of this principle of seedtime and harvest in Creation!

   Look at Genesis 1:11,12,21,24,25,29.

   In creation, we see God instituting the very law of the seed in the plants, in the animals and in mankind. The seed that was in every herb, every fruit tree and every creature that God created was designed to produce "after his kind." For example, not only would seed of the fruit tree produce a particular fruit, the fruit would have within it more seeds that would produce more fruit which had seed in it — "after his kind," continually perpetuating itself. If you have a seed, you have the potential for a harvest. This is one of God's laws.

   If God promised to prosper our seed, what type of "seed" can we sow? Certainly, we understand the natural principle of sowing and reaping as it pertains to farming or gardening. We also see from a study of God's Word that "seed" is a type of the Word of God that we are to sow the Word in our hearts and allow it to produce a rich spiritual harvest in our lives. Is it possible to "sow" money "seeds" and to "reap" financial increase? Let's look at what the Word of God says about this matter of sowing and reaping money.

2. 2 Corinthians 8:1-24; 9:1-14

   This passage is dealing specifically with the subject of giving money. The believers in Macedonia had been generous in giving to the poor saints in Jerusalem, and Paul was commending and instructing them. He included a reference to God's laws of sowing and reaping right in the middle of these passages on financial giving! These are great passages to spend time meditating on. Let's take a look at this in more detail.

   In light of the context, how are we to sow, according to chapter 9, verse 6? _____
   _____

The law of seedtime and harvest is an interesting one, because we will reap exactly what we sow. The seed will produce after its kind. In the natural, if you sow corn, you will reap corn; if you sow beans, you will reap beans. In spiritual matters, if you sow mercy, you will reap mercy; if you sow love and kindness, you will reap love and kindness. If you sow material things, you can expect to reap material things. If you sow finances, you will reap finances. The seed always produces after its kind! We can't sow corn and expect to reap beans. We can't sow hatred and expect to reap love. By the same token, we can't expect to reap finances by sowing corn. Whatever we desire to reap is exactly what we must sow!

How are we to sow? _____

If we sow a little, what will we reap? _____

If we sow much, what will we reap? _____

This sounds like Luke 6:38; we shall reap according to the measure that we sow, or give. A sobering question to ask yourself is, how much have you reaped lately? (It's a reflection of what you have sown!) Another question you might want to ask yourself is, how much do you want to reap? Then you must sow proportionately. A farmer can't expect ten acres of wheat if he only sows one acre of seed. You have to sow "seed" in the measure that you want to reap a "harvest."

We see a principle of investment and a principle of increase at work here. First, by faith, we must invest our seed — our finances — and sow it into the work of God. This is the principle of investment — a faith investment. After an interval of time, we will reap bountifully. That's the principle of increase. We *always* reap more than we sow!

According to chapter 9, verse 7, how would you describe the type of sower (giver) whom God loves? _____

_____

According to chapter 9, verse 10, who gives us the seed to sow? _____

_____

What will God do to the seed we sow? _____

Not only will we be blessed with a bountiful return on our sowing, but God will use our seed to bless others. Our seed multiplies to bless those to whom we give it, and we also receive an increase on our seed. God's economy is a win/win situation for everyone who will cooperate with His plan!

3. Galatians 6:7-10

    What will a person reap? _____

If we sow selfishly, to our fleshy desires, what will we reap? _____

_____

If we sow unselfishly, to the Spirit's desire, what will we reap? _____

_____

Often, there is an interval of time between the sowing and the reaping. We don't always see a big financial harvest the day after we have sown financial seed. In verse 9, what are we encouraged to do? _____

What will happen "in due season" if we don't faint? _____

_____

At times, when we have sown finances into the kingdom of God, we must exercise faith and patience, not casting away our confidence. God will not be mocked; we will reap exactly what we have sown. But we must exercise patience, waiting for the "due season." Then we shall reap!

There have been occasions when we have sown financial seed by faith and have seen the increase immediately! There have also been times when we have sown financial or material seed as a consistent way of life, and it has seemed as though it has taken years to truly see the lifestyle of continually reaping become a reality in our lives. The most exciting, yet most difficult, thing is that we remain in faith and not faint, because in due season we *will* reap!

4. Ecclesiastes 11:4

    What type of person will not sow or reap? _____

    _____

Did you know that the conditions won't always seem conducive to sowing? You won't just always have an extra $1000 in your pocket to sow. Don't be moved by the winds of life or by the clouds that cast shadows. By faith, determine that you will sow and reap according to God's laws of seedtime and harvest!

E. GOD BLESSES THOSE WHO GIVE TO THE POOR

God cares about the poor. We see from the Word of God that there are those who are poor materially and those who are poor spiritually. We express God's love to both categories of poor people. In our study, we will concentrate on giving to those who are poor financially.

In the Old Testament, we see God's love for the poor and His promises of blessing to those who would give to the poor.

1. Deuteronomy 15:7-11

   What type of attitude are we to have toward the poor? _____

   _____

   How are we to treat the poor? _____

2. Psalm 41:1

   If you consider the poor, what will the Lord do for you? _____

   _____

3. Proverbs 19:17

   Have you ever thought about lending to the Lord? He that pities and gives to the poor is doing what? _____

   What will the Lord give you for everything you give to the poor? _____

   _____

4. Proverbs 22:9

   A person who is generous and gives to the poor shall be what? _____

   _____

5. Proverbs 28:27

   What shall he who gives to the poor not have? _____

6. Proverbs 31:20

   What does a virtuous woman do? _____

   _____

7. Isaiah 58:5-14

   Fasting food is a good spiritual discipline for the believer; but in this passage God describes another type of fast that pleases Him. Describe it, according to verses 6, 7 and 10. _____

   _____

   What is promised to those who participate in this type of fast? _____

   _____

In the New Testament, we see Jesus teaching us to give to the poor and to do it in a particular way.

8. Matthew 6:1-4

   How are we to give our gifts (alms) to the poor? _____

   ALMS: The Greek word translated "alms" is *eleemosune* (pronounced *el-eh-ay-mos-oo'-nay*).[2] Its meaning includes compassion exercised towards the poor, beneficence.

   How will God reward us? _____

9. Acts 10:1-4

   Describe Cornelius, according to verse 2. _____
   _____

   According to verse 4, what came up before God? _____

   Obviously, God heard Cornelius's prayers and saw his giving to the poor. As a result, Cornelius and his household were the first Gentile converts after the resurrection of Jesus Christ. He gave to the poor, lending to the Lord, and the Lord certainly repaid him!

10. Acts 20:35

    What did Jesus say? _____

    When we participate in God's economy, we can see that we will be blessed abundantly! When we bring our tithes to God's storehouse; when we honor Him with our wealth; when we give offerings to His works and operate in His laws of sowing and reaping; and when we give alms to the poor; we can expect God to bless us financially!

F. PERSONAL APPLICATION

Perhaps you need to take some time to reflect, to pray and to consecrate yourself to be a doer of the Word in this area. Ask yourself these questions:

1. Am I consistent to tithe 10 percent of my income?

   - Do I "bring" all the tithe to my local church?

   - Am I tithing the "full" 10 percent?

   - Is my conscience clear on whether I tithe on the gross or on the net of my income?

2. Am I honoring God with the first fruits of all my increase?

   • Do I give the first fruits of my increase to the Lord?

   • Do I honor God by giving to my earthly parents?

   • Do I honor God by giving to those who are my spiritual parents?

3. Am I giving offerings to the work of God?

   • Are there special funds at my local church to which I could be giving offerings, such as building funds and missions funds?

   • Are there ministers, missionaries, ministries or other outreaches of the Gospel with whom I could become a monthly partner? If so, who?

   As food for thought, many ministries operate on monthly and annual budgets. It would be a great blessing to them if they knew they could count on your monthly support for an entire year. If you have never supported anyone on a monthly basis with your offerings, why not consider becoming a partner with a fruitful ministry?

   • Is there a certain amount of money you could designate each month to give toward offerings, then trust and expect the Lord to lead you? If so, how much?

4. Am I operating in God's laws of sowing and reaping?

   • Am I regularly sowing financially through my tithes and offerings?

   • Am I sowing in the measure that I would like to reap?

   • Have I considered sowing things other than money, such as my time, my talents or material things?

   • Am I exercising patience as I trust God, knowing that I shall reap if I faint not?

5. Am I giving to the poor?

   • Do I know any poor people to whom I could give a secret gift? If so, who?

   • Are there ministries that are specifically tending to the poor which I could support with my finances? If so, who?

CHAPTER EIGHT

"NO GET-RICH-QUICK SCHEME"
WHAT DOES GOD EXPECT FROM US?

The prosperity message has been criticized as a "get-rich-quick scheme" with a Christian spin. It has been stereotyped as a message for "lazy, faith Christians" who want to lay around watching TV while believing God to send money to them through the mail. The prosperity message has been resisted by some who think it advocates negligence in the areas of stewardship, wisdom and diligence. Unfortunately, such misunderstandings have caused numerous Christians to be robbed of the true Biblical plan God has for the prosperity of His people!

By now, having studied through this workbook, you've discovered that the prosperity message is definitely not a "get-rich-quick scheme." It isn't a message that exalts laziness and extreme faith. Neither is it a message that neglects the importance of true faith, stewardship, wisdom and diligence.

God's Word is rich with truth after truth about God's desire for His children to prosper! When we look at the example of the Old Testament saints; when we understand our Covenant and the prosperity that included the blessing of Abraham for New Testament believers; when we realize that God wants us to be blessed without apology; and when our motives for prosperity are ultimately for the advancement of God's kingdom; we can't help but get excited about God's goodness and richness toward us!

We have a part to play if we are to experience the prosperous life God intends for us to have. We must cooperate with His economic laws, and we must walk in the light of God's Word to qualify for the blessings of prosperity. We will be looking at four practical things God expects us to do.

A. WE MUST USE OUR FAITH

While there have been some extreme ideas concerning faith in the area of prosperity, there is nonetheless a truth we need to understand. As with everything we receive from God, we receive it by grace through faith. We must have faith to receive the greatest gift of all, our salvation, as well as all the other promises of God. In this area of prosperity, when we mix faith with the Word of God which we have studied, it will profit us! We aren't going to study in great detail the subject of faith in this chapter, but there are many good books on this subject; I recommend that you make it a practice to study the subject of faith from God's Word.

1.　James 1:5-8

According to verse 5, what can we ask God for? _____

When we ask God for it, in what way are we to ask? _____

If we ask God for wisdom, in faith, what can we expect, according to verse 5? _____
_____
_____

If we doubt or waver, what can we expect? (v. 7.) _____
_____
_____

Describe what it means to be double-minded. _____
_____

Now this passage is specifically referring to our need and request for wisdom, and we certainly need wisdom to prosper! The principle of faith described here is true. Whether we are requesting wisdom or any other promise from God's Word, including prosperity, we must ask God in faith — without wavering!

2.　Hebrews 4:2

The Gospel is good news. Through Jesus Christ and His shed blood, we have been redeemed from sin and death, from sickness and disease — and from poverty! Once we have heard God's Word about a particular aspect of the Gospel, we must act on what we have heard.

The Gospel did not profit some people because the Word they heard was not mixed with what? _____

You can hear and study what the Word of God says until you are well versed in the knowledge of that Word. But until you choose to mix faith with that knowledge, your knowledge of the Word will never profit you. Think about that. Based upon what you have studied in the Bible on the subject of prosperous living, do you now believe (have faith) that prosperity is indeed God's will for you? Are you willing to act according to your faith? If so — it will profit you!

3.　James 2:14-19

We must obtain the knowledge of God's will by studying His Word. For it to profit us, we must mix faith with the Word we have heard and with the knowledge we have received. True faith will have corresponding actions.

Let's take a look at this area of acting on our faith.

If a person says he has faith but does not have works or actions that substantiate his faith, will it profit him? _____

According to verse 17, faith without works is what? _____

In verse 18, how did James say he would show his faith? _____
_____

Consider these examples:

- If we have faith based upon God's Word, then actions are the natural result of true faith. A person who does not act on his faith really doesn't have faith at all; his faith is dead, and it will not profit him. How true this is in the area of prosperous living!

- If a person says he has faith in God and in His Word and is believing God to prosper him, but doesn't act on the most basic prosperity principle of the tithe — then he is really fooling himself. His faith is dead!

- If a person says he has faith in God and His Word and is believing God to prosper him, but his constant confession is about lack, about being in debt, about barely making ends meet — then again his faith is dead, and it will not profit him!

- If a person says he has faith in God and His Word and is believing God to prosper him, but the first time a financial storm blows his way, he falls apart and begins to doubt God's Word — then he becomes double-minded and is tossed to and fro. The Bible tells us that person should not expect to receive anything of the Lord.

- If a person says he has faith in God and in His Word and is believing God to prosper him; and if he chooses to be a good steward over what God has given him; chooses to walk in wisdom and to be diligent in his vocation; and if he is consistent and obedient in his tithing and in sowing seed — it's obvious that his actions back up his beliefs. If you watch that person long enough, you will see him begin to profit!

Can you see that we must act according to our faith? Do you believe God's Word and His promises concerning prosperity? In what ways are you acting on your faith?

Let's look at something else God expects of us if we are to prosper.

B. WE MUST BE GOOD STEWARDS

We have the responsibility to be a good steward, or we could say a good manager, over all God entrusts us with. In fact, if we will be good stewards with what God gives us, He will give us more!

Everything belongs to God. He is the Creator of the ends of the earth, and we are simply stewards for Him. In this chapter, we want to look at what God has entrusted to our care. As it relates to prosperity, we will look specifically at our responsibility to be good managers of our life, of our time, of the gifts and talents God has given us and of our money.

1. We are called to be stewards:

    1 Corinthians 4:1,2

    As believers in Christ, what are we are to be stewards over? _____
    _____

    We are to be good stewards over the mysteries of God, particularly the mystery of the Gospel, making them known to others! (Eph. 3:4,9; Col. 1:26,27.)

    What is required of stewards? _____

    Faithful to do what? _____

2. We must acknowledge that God owns everything:

    a. Psalm 24:1

        Who owns the earth and all that is in it? _____

    b. Psalm 50:10-12

        What belongs to God? _____
        _____

    c. Psalm 89:11

        What does God own? _____

    d. 1 Corinthians 6:19,20

        To whom do we belong? Who bought us? _____

        We can see that God owns everything — the world and all that's in it, including us! We are to be good stewards over God's creation and all He entrusts to our care.

3. We must manage our lives:

a. Luke 12:41-48

According to verse 42, what type of stewards are we to be? _____
_____

What will be the reward for the steward who is faithful and wise? _____
_____

What will be the reward for the steward who is unfaithful and unwise? _____
_____

b. Matthew 25:14-30

In this parable of the talents, we see Jesus expecting His servants to be profitable.

Describe what the three servants were given:

SERVANT #1 was given: _____

SERVANT #2 was given: _____

SERVANT #3 was given: _____

The talents were given to these servants according to their ability. What has God given you according to your ability? _____
_____

Describe the profit each servant made on the talents his master had given him:

SERVANT #1: _____

SERVANT #2: _____

SERVANT #3: _____

What about you? Have you multiplied the talents (gifts, abilities, advantages, wealth, time) God has given you? If so, how? If not, why not? _____
_____
_____

When the master of the servants came to reckon the accounts, what did he say to each of his servants?

SERVANT #1: _____
_____

SERVANT #2: _____

_____

SERVANT #3: _____

_____

If Jesus were to return today, what would He say to you regarding the use of your talents? _____

_____

4. We must manage our time:

Each one of us is given twenty-four hours a day to invest in a profitable way. What does God's Word say about our use of time?

a. Psalm 90:10,12

According to verse 10, how many years could be available to us? _____

According to verse 12, what are we to ask the Lord to help us do? _____

_____

Have you asked Him to do this in your life? _____

b. Proverbs 16:9

Who plans our way? _____

Who directs our steps? _____

c. 1 Corinthians 9:24-27

A good manager of his time is a disciplined person!

According to verse 24, how are we to run our race? _____

_____

To really excel, what must a person be? _____

_____

Describe what verses 26 and 27 are talking about as it relates to discipline and its application to the management of our time. _____

_____

d. Ephesians 5:15-17

How are we to walk? _____

How are we not to walk? _____

What do you think it means to "redeem the time"? _____
_____

To be a good manager of your time, you must understand verse 17. What does "understanding the will of the Lord" have to do with managing your time? _____
_____

e. 1 Samuel 12:21; Jeremiah 2:8

These passages describe people who did not use their time wisely. What do we learn about the things on which they spent their time? _____
_____

How do you spend your time? Are you living as a wise and sensible person in redeeming your time? How much time do you waste each day? If you don't already use some type of time management system, whether it be a professional planner or a pad of legal paper, I highly recommend that you begin to use some type of systematic plan for managing your time. Many companies and office supply stores offer a variety of paper and computer planners and calendars which will help you to get control of your time.

If you are one of those who has always said, *I'm just not organized*, then it's time you changed your confession of faith. Having studied these few Scriptures, we see that God has commanded us to be organized in managing our time. So you *can* do it! (There are many good books on time management and I recommend you read along this line if this is an area of weakness in your life.)

5. We must manage our God-given gifts and talents:

a. Romans 11:29

What is God not going to change His mind about? _____
_____

God has gifted and called us after His own plan. He will not repent, or change His mind, about the gifts and callings He has placed upon your life. It would be wise for you as a good steward to identify your gifts and callings, then to fulfill them!

b. Romans 12:3-8

According to verse 6, do we all have the same gifts? _____

God has given us His grace to function in the gifts He has given us. Think about it this way: God has "graced" you with the ability to do certain things. Because of God's "gracing," it's easy and almost natural for you to function in certain areas. To be a wise steward, you must recognize God's grace in your life and identify the different gifts He has given you!

c. 1 Corinthians 1:7; 7:7; 12:1,4,31; Ephesians 3:7; 4:7,8

The apostle Paul talks much about gifts among the body of believers. We see from these Scriptures that there are a variety of gifts. What various types of gifts can you identify from these passages? _____
_____
_____

d. 1 Timothy 4:14; 2 Timothy 1:6

According to these verses, how are some gifts given? _____
_____

What are we to do with these gifts? _____
_____

e. 1 Peter 4:10

Who has received a gift? _____

To be good stewards, what are we to do with the gift(s) we receive from God? _____
_____

We are to use our gifts so that who may be glorified? _____
_____

God has given us gifts and callings for a reason. If we will recognize and identify our gifts and callings, then be diligent to stir them up and use them as good stewards of the manifold grace of God, we will be blessed, and others will be blessed, and God will be glorified.

f. Deuteronomy 28:8

What has God promised if we put our hand (our gifts and callings) to work? _____
_____

Do you know what your gifts and callings are? Have you prepared yourself so that you will be able to maximize their use in your life? Are you currently using your gifts and functioning in your calling to their full or partial capacity? Do you recognize that God is continuing to hone and to refine your gifts and callings as you exercise them? Do you believe you are a good steward of the grace with which God has gifted you? Is God being glorified through the use of your gifts and callings? As you use your gifts and callings, do you see God prospering that to which you put your hand?

6. We must manage our money:

a. Luke 16:9-13

According to verse 9, what are we to do? _____

_____

What do you think this is a reference to? _____

_____

We are told here to manage and to invest our money in such a way as to win for God the souls of the unrighteous ones. We are to use our money to win friends for Christ; then should they die before we do, they will be waiting in heaven to receive us when we get there! What a grand reunion — to meet and be welcomed by hundreds and thousands of people who are in heaven because you were a good manager of your money. They are there because you used your wealth to see to it that more and more people were won to Christ!

In verse 11, we are told to be faithful in what area of life? _____

_____

If we are not faithful in managing money (unrighteous mammon), then God is saying He cannot entrust us with true riches; that is, spiritual things. In other words, in verses 10 and 11, God is saying that, if we can't be faithful in managing something as measly as money, which is the least, then how can we be trusted with something as weighty as spiritual truth, which is worth much more?

b. Luke 14:28

How should a wise builder manage his money in this verse? _____

_____

C. WE MUST USE WISDOM

God expects us to walk in His wisdom. There are too many Christians who have jumped on the "prosperity bandwagon" and who have prayed, believed and confessed prosperity without using one ounce of wisdom! The result is numerous people who are disillusioned, skeptical, burnt out and leery of the prosperity message.

It seems many sincere and well-meaning Christians need a healthy dose of God's wisdom when it comes to implementing His plan for prosperity in their lives. In fact, when studying this subject, we will find that as we operate in the wisdom of God, prosperity is the natural by-product. We can't help but prosper if we walk in God's wisdom. So let's look at this subject.

1. Prayer for wisdom:

   James 1:5-8

   We have already looked at this passage, but let's take a moment to review.

   For what can we ask God? _____

   If we, in faith, ask God to give us His wisdom to prosper according to His plan, will He give it to us? _____

2. Examples of those who through wisdom prospered:

   a. Joseph, Samuel and David

   Take time to read these passages and write down your observations of the relationship between the wisdom God had given to these men and their prosperity and success:

   Joseph: Genesis 37:2-17; 39:3-9; 41:38

   _____
   _____
   _____
   _____

   Samuel: 1 Samuel 2:26; 3:1-21; 7:3-17

   _____
   _____
   _____

   David: 1 Samuel 16:11-13; 17:12-58; 18:1-7

   _____
   _____
   _____
   _____

b. Solomon

To understand what God means when He says He is going to give someone riches and wealth, we must look at the life of Solomon one of the wisest men that ever lived and see what God did for him. Solomon's life is a testimony of God's definition of riches and wealth. (Refer to Chapter 1 for a detailed study on Solomon's wealth.)

2 Chronicles 1:7-15

God appeared unto Solomon one night and said to him, **Ask what I shall give thee** (v. 7).

What was Solomon's response in verse 10? _____

_____

God was pleased with Solomon's request for wisdom and with the motives of his heart. What was God's response to Solomon's request, according to verses 11 and 12?

_____

_____

Solomon asked for wisdom, and he received wisdom, as well as riches and wealth. The next time you wonder if God wants you to have wisdom and wealth at the same time, just remember King Solomon!

c. Daniel

We won't be studying Daniel's life in depth, but we do want to look at the connection between the wisdom Daniel had and the success and prosperity he experienced as the result.

Study Daniel 1:1-21; 2:14-23,27-30,46-49; 5:11-14; 6:1-5,25-28.

According to chapter 1, verses 4, 17, 20; and chapter 5, verses 11-14, how is Daniel described? _____

_____

_____

In chapter 2, verses 14, 20, 21, 23, 28 and 30, who did Daniel say had given him wisdom? _____

What was the result of operating in God's wisdom, according to chapter 2, verses 46-49, and chapter 6, verses 1-3 and 25-28? _____

_____

_____

Would you call this prosperity? _____

3. Wisdom and prosperity in the book of Proverbs:

We find over and over in the book of Proverbs the exhortation to seek after wisdom, to follow wisdom, to desire and to exalt wisdom in our lives. As we shall see, promotion, prosperity, wealth, riches and the knowledge of witty inventions comes with wisdom. If we find that prosperous living is the by-product of living in wisdom, then we would do well to study this subject.

First, we must ask the questions: *What is wisdom? How is it defined?* Proverbs 9:10 tells us, **The fear of the Lord is the beginning of wisdom.** So, without reverence for the Lord and His Word, a person cannot even begin to have wisdom.

WISDOM: Let's look at seven Hebrew words that are translated *wisdom* in the book of Proverbs:

- *chokmah* means wisdom, in a good sense, skillful, wisely, wit.[1]

- *biynah* means understanding, knowledge, wisdom.[2]

- *leb* is sometimes translated wisdom.[3]

- `ormah* means shrewdness, trickery, or in a good sense, discretion, prudence, wisdom.[4]

- *sakal* means circumspect, intelligent, prudence, skillful understanding, and wisdom.[5]

- *sekel* means intelligence, success, discretion, knowledge, prudence, sense, understanding, and wisdom.[6]

- *tuwshiyah*, or, *tushiaya* means ability, help, understanding, and sound wisdom.[7]

If we were to summarize the definition of wisdom based upon these seven Hebrew words, we could say that godly, biblical wisdom is a combination of discernment, discrimination, knowledge, understanding, shrewdness, subtlety, prudence, good sense, intelligence and discretion. This certainly is something to meditate upon!

a. Proverbs 3:13-18

A person is happy if he finds what? _____

The merchandise of wisdom and understanding is better than what four things?

_____   _____

_____   _____

What is in wisdom's right hand? _____

What is in wisdom's left hand? _____

b. Proverbs 4:5-9

According to verses 5-7, what are we to do in relation to wisdom? _____
_____

What is the principal thing? _____

What happens to us if we exalt wisdom? _____
_____

Would you consider promotion a part of the prosperous life? _____

c. Proverbs 8:10-12

What is better than silver, choice gold, rubies and all the things you could desire?
_____

According to verse 12, wisdom dwells with prudence and finds out what? _____
_____

How would you define a "witty invention?" _____
_____

Do you realize that one "witty invention" from God, just one idea that stems out of wisdom, could make you a millionaire? (We will be studying this subject in more detail in the next chapter.)

d. Proverbs 8:17-21

We are to love wisdom and to seek wisdom early. If we do, what will be the result?
_____

To seek wisdom early could have a twofold application. First, we ought to seek God's wisdom early each day. Second, we ought to seek wisdom early in our lifetime, and we ought to encourage those who are young to do the same. There is tremendous potential for the young person who seeks God's wisdom in his or her early years!

According to verse 18, what is with wisdom? _____
_____

What does verse 19 tell us about the fruit of wisdom? _____
_____

In verse 21, what does wisdom cause us to inherit? _____
_____

e. Proverbs 9:1-6; 24:3,4

We see evidence of what wisdom is able to provide in terms of prosperity and blessing. In these passages, what do you see wisdom doing? _____
_____
_____

f. Proverbs 14:24

What type of crown is evidence that a person is wise? _____
_____

g. Proverbs 16:16

What is better than gold or silver? _____

Why do you think this is true? _____
_____

From what we have studied so far, it is clear that if you have wisdom you will automatically have riches, gold, silver and treasures!

h. Proverbs 21:20

What is to be found in the home of a wise person? _____
_____

How would you describe this in modern terms? _____
_____

It is clear from this study in Proverbs that prosperity is the by-product of walking in wisdom. Over and over, we see that wealth, riches and treasures are found in the life of the wise person. On the other side of the coin, we must be honest with ourselves and realize that if we aren't experiencing riches and wealth as a regular occurrence in our lives, perhaps we need to be more diligent to walk in wisdom. I realize this is a sobering thought. But from what we have just studied in Proverbs, it's a thought worth meditating on and praying about. Thank God, mercy and grace are always available for us to make adjustments and to go from glory to glory in His perfect will!

D. WE MUST BE DILIGENT IN OUR WORK

To prosper in life, we must be diligent in our work. For some, this sounds like the pin that bursts the "prosperity bubble." We are to use our faith, to be good stewards of all God has given us, to walk in wisdom and to be diligent in our work. The Bible is full of exhortations and promises of prosperity to those who will be diligent, who will put their hand to the plow and labor. The Bible is also full of warnings of poverty to those who aren't diligent, but who are lazy, slothful or sluggards!

Very often we have the wrong idea about work. For many people, work is something to dread, to endure and to get through so that their weekend can be enjoyed. Unfortunately, a person with that attitude is robbed of enjoying forty-plus hours of his life each week! Did God intend for our work to be something we despise? So many times we have viewed work as the punishment that resulted from the curse of sin. But as we study the Bible, we will find that work and labor were a part of God's original plan for man. Certainly, sin brought some difficulties to our labor. But work was and is a part of God's original design!

Let's study this very important subject of diligence and work.

1. God is our example of a diligent worker:

    a. Genesis 1:1-5,7,16,17,21,22,25,27; 2:1

    In creation, before sin ever entered the scene, we see God at work! What phrases or words are used to describe the type of work God did in these verses? _____

    _____

    _____

    b. Genesis 1:4,10,12,18,21,25,31

    God took pride in His work! A sense of enjoyment and accomplishment was evident as God saw what He had created. What phrase is used to describe the quality of all that God had made?

    c. Genesis 2:2,3

    What did God do on the seventh day? _____

    From what did He take a rest? _____

    d. Genesis 1:26,27

    In whose image and likeness were we created? _____

If in creation, we see God was a worker who enjoyed the accomplishment of a job well done, and if we are created in His image and likeness, would it make sense that we were created to be workers who enjoy the sense of accomplishment of a job well done?

e. Genesis 2:15

After man was created, before sin ever entered the human race, what was he commissioned by God to do? _____

_____

God told Adam to work! He was given orders to dress and to keep the Garden of Eden. Let's look at these two words: *dress* and *keep.*

DRESS: The Hebrew word for "dress" is `abad (pronounced *aw-bad'*), which means to work, serve, till, labor, work, and serve.[8]

KEEP: The Hebrew word for "keep" is *shamar* (pronounced *shaw-mar'*).[9] Its meaning includes to hedge about, to keep, guard, observe, attend, preserve, and watch.

Work was a part of God's original design for man. It was not just the "cruel result and aftermath of sin." God wanted man to experience the enjoyment and the sense of accomplishment of a job well done. Just as God enjoyed viewing His creation and saw "that it was good," so too man could enjoy his work and labor and, with a sense of satisfaction, could see "that it was good."

f. John 4:34; 5:17; 9:4; 17:4

Jesus Christ Himself worked! Read these passages and describe Jesus' view and example of work. _____

_____

_____

2. What the Bible says about work and labor:

a. Psalm 104:22,23

What does man do from morning to evening? _____

b. Psalm 128:1,2

What will you do with the labor of your hands? _____

c. Proverbs 10:16

What do the righteous do that tends toward life? _____

d. Proverbs 13:11

If you want wealth that increases, how do you obtain it? _____

_____

e. Proverbs 14:23

If you want to profit, where is it found? _____

What do those who are "all talk and no work" receive? _____

_____

f. Proverbs 21:25

What will happen to the person who refuses to labor? _____

_____

What is this type of person called? _____

g. Ecclesiastes 1:1,3; 2:24; 3:13; 5:18,19; 8:15

The author concludes that while society operates on the basis of profit and loss, apart from God's purpose, it is all meaningless. He summarizes in these passages that the person who eats, drinks, is merry and enjoys his labor has received the gift of God.

What does Solomon tell us about enjoying our labor? _____

_____

_____

h. Acts 20:33-35; 1 Thessalonians 2:9; 2 Thessalonians 3:8

The apostle Paul was an example of a Christian who labored both in the natural and in ministry. We see that he was a hard worker and a diligent laborer for the Lord. Describe Paul's work ethic. _____

_____

_____

i. Ephesians 4:28

Is it right for a Christian to steal? _____

If a person is able to work but chooses not to, in what ways can he or she "steal?"

_____

If this person lacks money, what is he or she supposed to do? _____

_____

A person who labors and works will not only earn enough money to take care of himself, but will have extra money to do what? _____

_____

j. 1 Thessalonians 4:11,12

What four things did the Holy Spirit, through the apostle Paul, urge these Christians to do?

_____

_____

_____

_____

k. 2 Thessalonians 3:10-12

What did the Holy Spirit, through the apostle Paul, command concerning those who would not work? _____

_____

Describe the type of person pictured in verse 11. _____

_____

_____

This is a description of what we might call a freeloader — the type of person who won't work, who wants to stick his nose into other people's business — and who expects others to foot the bill for his existence. Unfortunately, even in Christian circles there are people who fit this description. Rather than exercising diligence and obeying the command to work, they make excuses for their laziness and freeload off of others. It's wise to be aware of this type of personality.

Some lazy people are so good at being a con artist that they make other people feel guilty for not supporting them. They make themselves out to be poor, and their misuse of a few Scriptures and guilt causes others to feel sorry for them to the degree that they get handouts. What these people really need to do is to repent and to get a job! They need to obey this command of Scripture and go to work. (We will look at the description of the sluggard later in this chapter.)

This type of person is commanded and exhorted by the Lord Jesus Christ to do what?

_____

Whose bread is he supposed to eat? _____

3. Words for employees and employers:

a. Psalm 123:2

   We see a parallel between the employee/employer relationship and our relationship with God.

   What do we trust God to do for us? _____

   _____

   What does an employee trust his employer to do for him/her? _____

   _____

b. Ephesians 6:5-8; Colossians 3:22-24; 1 Timothy 6:1,2; Titus 2:9,10; 1 Peter 2:18

   In New Testament times, the words *master* and *servants* were used frequently to depict what we commonly refer to as employer and employee.

   According to these verses, list all the things an employee is supposed to do. _____

   _____

   _____

   _____

   As an obedient employee, who is your real boss or employer? _____

   As an employee, you are serving Christ; what will the Lord do for you? _____

   _____

   According to 1 Timothy 6:2, how are you to behave if your employer is a believer? __

   _____

   According to 1 Peter 2:18, if your employer doesn't behave as a Christian, what are you to do? _____

   _____

   Christians ought to be the best workers in the world! Whether your employer is Christian or non-Christian, your work ethic, diligence, honesty and integrity should be a testimony of your Christianity!

c. Ephesians 6:9; Colossians 4:1

   How are employers to treat their employees? _____

   _____

4. The blessing of prosperity for being diligent:

Do you realize the responsibility you have for your prosperity? In other words, do you realize that to some degree the ball is your court in certain areas of the prosperity equation?

Don't be like some Christians who are waiting for God to just plop down prosperity at their doorstep. The potential for prosperity is available to every Christian if they will just be diligent. There is no such thing as a lifestyle of idleness where prosperity just magically falls down on you from heaven! Unfortunately, many Christians have been deceived by the devil in this area, thinking that somehow prosperity would be bequeathed to them. As I pointed out earlier, they see it much the same as in the story of Peter Pan, where Tinkerbell spread magic dust on those who were to be blessed. But God isn't like Tinkerbell! We have a responsibility to obey the Bible and to cooperate with God's laws for prosperity — and diligence is one of those laws. If we are diligent, then we can qualify for the blessings of prosperity!

a. Proverbs 10:4

What type of person becomes rich? _____

What type of person becomes poor? _____

b. Proverbs 12:24

Who becomes the ruler, the leader, the promoted? _____

What happens to the slothful? _____

c. Proverbs 12:27

What is the slothful man too lazy to do? _____

_____

What does the diligent man have? _____

d. Proverbs 13:4

The sluggard wants to prosper, but what does he get? _____

_____

What happens to the diligent? _____

e. Proverbs 21:5

What does a diligent person think about? _____

f. Proverbs 22:29

What will happen to a person who is diligent in his business or field? _____
_____

g. Proverbs 27:23

What are we to be diligent in? _____

How would you state this in modern terms? _____
_____

Can you see that there is the promise of prosperity to those who will be diligent? In what areas would you consider yourself to be diligent? In what areas of work or business or ministry could you be more diligent?

5. The curse of poverty for the sluggard:

It is no compliment to be called lazy or slothful or a sluggard. This is a title to be avoided! Let's take a look at what the Bible says about the poverty of the lazy person, taking heed to ourselves to be sure we don't fall into this category.

a. Proverbs 6:6-11 (see also Prov. 20:13; 23:21)

The sluggard can look at the ant, consider her ways and be wise. What can we learn from the ant? _____
_____
_____

What was the downfall of the sluggard? In other words, what lust of the flesh hindered him? _____
_____

Although our bodies certainly need sleep and rest, too much sleep can cause us to become like the lazy sluggard. Determine how much sleep you need to function to your optimum, and avoid oversleeping.

According to verse 11 (also Prov. 20:13; 23:21), what will come upon those who spend too much time sleeping?

b. Proverbs 15:19

What kinds of things does a lazy person encounter or imagine are in his path? _____
_____

A lazy person always makes excuses for his laziness and his unproductive life.

c. Proverbs 18:9

The person who is slothful in his work is a brother to whom? _____
_____

A lazy person wastes time, materials and resources because he is not efficient, disciplined, organized or a good steward.

d. Proverbs 19:24

A slothful person is too lazy to do what? _____
_____

e. Proverbs 20:4

The sluggard is full of excuses. When it's time to reap the harvest, what excuse does the sluggard have for not working in the field? _____
_____

If a person doesn't reap when it's harvest time, what will be the result? _____
_____

f. Proverbs 22:13

The slothful person won't be productive because of unrealistic fears and excuses. What did the lazy person say in this verse? _____
_____

g. Proverbs 24:30-34

Describe the field and vineyard of the slothful. _____
_____
_____

According to verse 32, this writer received instruction by observation. What did he learn in verses 33 and 34?

Have you observed, considered well and received instruction as you have looked upon the life of a person who is lazy? What have you learned? _____
_____
_____

h. Proverbs 26:13-16

What four traits of a lazy person are listed in this passage?

_____

_____

_____

_____

It's interesting to note that a lazy person is full of pride. Seven people with reason cannot convince this lazy person of his error because of his pride.

i. Matthew 25:26-28

Jesus had strong words for the slothful servant. How did Jesus describe him? _____

_____

j. Romans 12:11

When it comes to our business, work or service, what are we not to be? _____

_____

k. Hebrews 6:10-12

In speaking about our work and labor for the Lord, what are we told, according to verse 10? _____

_____

Concerning diligence and slothfulness in following and serving the Lord, what are we told to do in verses 11 and 12? _____

_____

E. PERSONAL APPLICATION

What does your own financial balance sheet look like?

When it comes to financial management, we need to exercise wisdom and good judgment.

There are many good books written by Christian ministers who have had success in financial matters, just as have bankers, financial planners and consultants. Their books are worth reading. In these books, in addition to walking in God's economic laws as outlined in this workbook, you can learn in more detail about the spiritual power you have to rebuke the devil and to commission angels in the area of your finances. You can also learn wisdom about natural things, such as budgeting, borrowing, credit and debt, investments, building equity, and even more. It's wise to seek the knowledge and wisdom of counsel from people in this area so that you can stay on top of your financial state of affairs.

You must seek first God's kingdom (Matt. 6:33), not trusting in uncertain riches, but in God. You must use your faith (Mark 11:23,24) and be a good steward of all God has given you. You must obey God and His Word (Isa. 1:19) in tithing, in giving offerings and in operating the laws of sowing and reaping. You must be led by the Spirit (Rom. 8:14) and walk in wisdom. When you do these things, your debt will be reduced and your income will increase. Then you will be living proof to others that prosperous living is indeed God's will for His children. It may not happen overnight; but as you stay faithful to God's economic laws, you will come out on top!

CHAPTER NINE

"THE SKY IS THE LIMIT"
EXPANDING YOUR VISION FOR PROSPEROUS LIVING

Are you convinced that God wants you to prosper? Hopefully by now you are convinced! Not only does He want you to prosper in this life, He wants you to prosper in a big way!

In this workbook, we have studied the subject of prosperous living from various vantage points. We have looked at the definition of prosperity. We have examined many misunderstandings and common questions people have when it comes to prosperous living. We have studied the life of Jesus to find out He really wasn't poor like many have traditionally thought Him to be. We have seen prosperity as part of God's original plan — as part of His Covenant with man — with prosperity revealed in the lives of God's people in the Bible. We have also dealt with the subject of our motives and the purpose for prosperity. We have looked at God's economy and what we should expect from God as we cooperate with His laws of giving and receiving. We have seen what God expects from us in terms of faith, stewardship, wisdom, diligence and our responsibility to work. We have taken a look at the big picture on prosperous living. Now, in conclusion, we want to expand our thinking just a bit more.

God has a big plan for your life! He will use you to reach a potential as big as you will believe Him for! He has more creative and innovative ways of using you and of prospering you than you could ever imagine. You must break out of the traditional, small, average, everyday, "life as usual" type of thinking. These are days to think beyond yourself, to think about life, finances and the Gospel from God's perspective! God wants to enlarge you. He wants your influence for Him to be enlarged. He wants your finances to be enlarged. We must think big, "enlarged" thoughts!

In these last days, it's imperative that the Body of Christ, and individual believers, prosper financially and materially. We need wealth and riches to get the Gospel out to the entire world! We must not allow the devil to talk us out of it! I believe when God finds a man or woman with the right heart, with the right motives and purpose and who cooperates with His economic laws, He is able to use them for His glory and to bless them with wealth exceedingly and abundantly above and beyond all they could ask or think. (Eph. 3:20.) God wants His people and His kingdom to prosper in a big way!

This may sound a bit exaggerated, and I am speaking somewhat fictitiously. But based upon our study, in thinking of God's desire to prosper His people, it seems to me that a born-again Christian has one of two possible callings in life. Let's consider these two possibilities.

Number one possibility: a believer could be called to serve God in full-time ministry and to use all of his or her time, talents and resources for assisting or for preaching the Gospel of the Lord Jesus Christ around the world.

Number two possibility: a believer could be called by God to accumulate wealth and give millions and millions of dollars to the work of the Gospel around the world!

So, which one are you? Maybe both? We have to think BIG! God wants us to be busy about His business, telling the world about His Son Jesus Christ. That takes lots of Christians preaching the Gospel and lots of Christians giving thousands and thousands of dollars to Gospel ministry works!

In this chapter, we want to expand our thinking a little and study the possibilities.

A. ARE YOU GOING TO REACH YOUR GOD-GIVEN POTENTIAL?

Have you ever had feelings of worthlessness? Failure? Despair? Have you been attacked by the "I can'ts," the "Who cares?" or the "That's impossible" syndrome? Have you ever felt stupid? Unqualified? Like a reject? Do you ever feel like you're in a rut? Standing still? Going in circles? Spinning your wheels? Have you ever felt there was more for you to do for God? To achieve in life?

Would you like to reach your greatest God-given potential? In life? In ministry? In finances? In relationships? God has a wonderfully fulfilling and fruitful plan for your life. In this chapter, we want to take a look at how we can reach our God-given potential.

Proverbs 29:18

Where there is no vision what happens? _____

A vision is like the flight plan that keeps the pilot on course with his destination. It's like the bull's-eye that gives the archer a target to shoot at. A vision is something to believe for, to reach for and to work for. A person without a vision wanders aimlessly through life. God wants you to get hold of His vision for your life! So let's begin to look at God's Word to see the vision He has for you.

1. God wants you to like yourself!

    First, God wants you to like yourself because, after all, He made you! What are you saying to God about His handiwork when you don't like yourself?

    In the secular world, phrases like "self-image" and "self-esteem" are used to describe how we see ourselves and how we measure our own worth. Whatever phraseology you prefer to use, our "self-image" in Christ and our "self-esteem" in Christ will be the blueprints by which we build the rest of our lives. If we wish to have a prosperous and successful life, we must begin with the right set of blueprints. That is, seeing ourselves as God sees us, in Christ, prosperous and successful, and believing that we are valuable in God's sight and worth being prospered. We will not prosper beyond how we see ourselves. So we must see ourselves as God sees us, and He sees us with incredible potential!

Perhaps because of ignorance, the cruelty of others, harsh words or experiences, you have developed a "self-image," or mental photograph of yourself, that isn't in line with how God sees you. It's possible to transform your "self-image" with new "photos!" Perhaps because of your background, you have developed a general feeling of worthlessness or a low self-esteem. Maybe you don't value yourself like you should, and like God does. It's possible to transform your self-esteem by going to God's Word.

a. Romans 12:2

   If we renew our minds to what God's Word says, what will happen to us? _____
   _____

b. Psalm 139:14-16

   What are we to praise God for? _____

   How did He make us? _____

   Does your soul (mind, emotions and will) know it full well? _____
   _____

c. Proverbs 23:7

   What does this tell us about what we think of ourselves? _____
   _____

This is true for Christians and non-Christians alike. What we think about ourselves is indeed what we become!

What do you think about yourself? Take a moment and write down at least five positive words or adjectives to describe how you view yourself. (Don't be embarrassed to use positive words; no one but you will read this!)

_____   _____

_____   _____

_____   _____

Here are some words to help get you started:

loving	kind	loyal	creative	leader
faithful	patient	joyful	peaceful	gentle
fun	funny	happy	positive	encourager
merciful	lovable	friendly	cooperative	sincere
successful	wise	teachable	generous	giving
organized	victorious	kind	creative	humble
enthusiastic	energetic	anointed	impacting	carefree

d. Romans 12:3

What are we not to think about ourselves? _____

_____

How are we to think about ourselves? _____

_____

Does this verse tell us to think lowly of ourselves? _____

To think soberly is simply to think in line with the truth about yourself, and the truth about each one of us is found in the Bible! God's Word says that we are more than conquerors through Christ, that we are to reign in life as kings and are to overcome the world through our faith. (Rom. 8:37; 5:17; 1 John 5:4.) Begin to think of yourself according to what God's Word says about you!

e. 2 Corinthians 10:12

God made you special. He has gifted and equipped you in a unique way! So stop comparing yourself to others. You aren't them — you are you!

What does this verse tell us is unwise? _____

_____

f. Matthew 22:36-40

What did Jesus say were the two greatest commandments? _____

_____

How are we to love our neighbor? _____

_____

What do you think of yourself?_____

Really, it doesn't matter what others think of you nearly as much as it matters what you think of you. Of course, we aren't talking about self-worship, which is to be narcissistic, or having an excessive love or admiration of oneself. We are talking about the healthy love you should have for yourself.

Do you accept yourself just as you are? _____

Would you say that you love yourself? _____

Would you rather be somebody else, or are you glad that you are you? _____

_____

Do you talk to or about yourself with respect or with ridicule? _____

_____

2. God wants you to see yourself a success!

   a. Joshua 1:8

      What was God's plan for those who would meditate upon His Word, speak His Word and do His Word? _____

      _____

      God's plan for you is success; He wants you to prosper in life!

   b. Jeremiah 29:10-14

      God always had a good plan for His people, Israel. When they were in captivity because of unbelief and rebellion, this Word came forth from the prophet Jeremiah — and God's heart for His people is still the same.

      According to verse 11, what kind of plan does God have for His people? _____

      _____

   c. 1 Corinthians 2:9-12

      According to verse 9, describe the things God has prepared for those who love Him.

      _____

      According to verses 10-12, is God keeping these things a secret? _____

      _____

By listening to the Spirit of God, what can we know? _____
_____
_____

d. Ephesians 3:20

What is God able to do in our lives? _____
_____

Do you believe God wants you to like yourself? Do you believe He has a good future planned for you? Like everything else in God's kingdom, you must believe these things by faith. Begin saying by faith what God says about you and about your future!

B. IS YOUR GOD TOO SMALL? THINK BIG!

I love the subject of thinking big. If anyone ought to think big, it ought to be Christians. If God is on our side, who can be against us? (Rom. 8:31.) With God, all things are possible! (Matt. 19:26.) Sure, it takes faith. Sure, it takes patience. But what a faith adventure we can have when we trust God for big things! Let's look at this subject.

1. With God, all things are possible:

To enjoy prosperity as a lifestyle, you must become a possibility thinker! To enjoy a prosperous lifestyle, you can't be negative, always seeing the glass half-empty. You must have that "never say die" tenacity. You have to use your faith and believe God to "find a way where there is no way." You have to get in the habit of just thinking of all the possibilities!

a. Matthew 19:26

What is possible with God? _____

b. Mark 9:23

If you will believe, what is possible to you? _____

c. Mark 10:27

What is possible with God? _____

d. Luke 1:37

With God, what is impossible? _____

e. Luke 18:27

What is possible with God? _____

f. Romans 8:31

If God is for us, who can be against us? _____

2. God will meet big faith:

a. 1 Chronicles 4:9,10

This story of Jabez is one that has always intrigued me. Jabez is an example of a person with big faith, and God honored him by answering his request!

What five things did Jabez ask God for?

_____   _____

_____   _____

_____

Jabez asked God to bless him in a big way!

What did God do? _____

b. Ephesians 3:20

What is God able to do? _____

_____

According to what power? _____

c. Philippians 4:13

What can you do? _____

Through what power? _____

Are you a big thinker? _____

Did you know that God can do amazing things with one person who will believe Him for big things? What is the biggest thought you have ever had? What is the highest expectation you have ever had for your life? Is it time for you to expand your thinking and to think a little bigger?

Place an "H" by the ideas you HAVE considered becoming a reality in your life and a "W" by those you WOULD consider:

_____running for public office

_____going to the moon

_____inventing something

_____recording a music CD

_____giving $50,000 to missions

_____being a public speaker

_____visiting the Holy Land

_____sending all your children to college

_____starting an outreach ministry to the poor

_____becoming president of the United States

_____becoming supervisor or manager where you work

_____traveling around the world

_____buying your parents or some other person a new car

_____having lunch with the governor of your state

_____becoming a professional athlete

_____personally leading someone to Jesus Christ

_____becoming a multi-millionaire

_____starting your own business

_____living to be 100 years old

_____writing a book

_____going to Bible school

_____flying an airplane

_____being a missionary

_____learning to use a computer and the Internet

_____laying hands on the sick and seeing them recover

_____learning to play a musical instrument

_____obtaining your Bachelor's, Master's or Ph.D.

_____influencing one million people for Jesus Christ in your lifetime

_____living in a 6,000-square-foot home

_____helping your church grow to reach 50,000 people

So, how big is your thinking? Obviously, in any of these things, you would have to be led by the Spirit. But the point of this exercise is to get you to expand your thinking and to break out of parameters that have held you back.

C. IS YOUR GOD TOO BORING AND PREDICTABLE? BE CREATIVE!

God is not boring! He is the most creative, invigorating, stimulating Person in all the universe! He is full of invention, innovation, discovery, surprises, blessings and revelation. Why then are so many Christians so predictable and boring? What does creativity look like?

Creativity is the ability to take nothing and make something. To take something and to make it better. To take something existing and to make it exciting. Creativity gives us products, conveniences, luxuries, cures, and more. Creativity motivates entrepreneurs, scientists, engineers, doctors and executives — and it should motivate us!

Creativity doesn't know that it can't. It doesn't believe in impossibility. It won't accept that it's too late. It won't take no for an answer, and it finds a way where there is no way. Creativity is faith in action! It is convinced that it can move mountains. It isn't limited by tradition, by boundaries or by narrow thinking. It just doesn't quit! Creativity doesn't pass life with time; it passes time with life. It doesn't wait for things to happen; it makes things happen. Creativity is found in motivators, pacesetters, pioneers and leaders. It's optimistic about the future, discontent with the status quo, highly curious and observant. It's a faith dreamer! Creativity — faith in action — is not limited to a select few who we traditionally think of as creative, like inventors, artists, sculptors, writers, or photographers. Anyone who will believe can be creative! We were made in God's image and likeness. He, the Creator, is the original Creative One!

So we need to tap into God's creative power! We have the Holy Spirit living on the inside of us, and we need to get to know Him a little better. He knows all of God's secrets and revelations, His treasures and mysteries. As we discover this facet of God, there is adventure and wealth!

Think about this for a moment: do you realize that everything which needs to be discovered, invented, uncovered, developed or modified has not yet been done? Just think of the vistas of creativity that have yet to be uncovered. In fact, all the inventions and discoveries that have been uncovered on earth so far have always potentially been here. For example, the potential for electricity was always here on the earth; hundreds of years before it was discovered, it was here! God created our world with the ability to have electricity from the beginning. Then one day someone discovered this wonderful part of God's creation, and people have been prospering from it ever since!

God has secrets to share. Discoveries to reveal. Innovation and invention to make known. Entrepreneurs to be born. Not every idea has been thought of yet! It just makes sense that Christians who are in fellowship with God should have the Creator of the world unlocking certain secrets of His creation to them, revealing secrets of the universe yet undiscovered!

Do you realize that it just takes one idea from God to put you on the financial map? Whether that idea be simply a brand-new invention, or an adaptation, or an improvement, or a modification of something already existing, one good idea from God can make you a millionaire!

By faith, all things are possible! Do you believe that? Do you see the possibilities? Would you like God to use you in the areas of invention, innovation or entrepreneurship? Let's see what the Bible says about God and His creativity.

1. Secrets, revelation and creativity:

    a. Deuteronomy 29:29

       What belongs to the Lord? _____

       What belongs to us? _____

    b. Psalm 25:14

       With whom will the Lord share His secrets? _____
       _____

    c. Proverbs 3:32

       God's secret is with whom? _____

    d. Isaiah 45:3

       What will God give? _____

       What is found in the darkness and secret places of God? _____
       _____
       _____

       Why does God give us "treasures of darkness" and "hidden riches of secret places"?
       _____

    e. Daniel 2:19,22,28-30

       What did God reveal to Daniel? _____

       What did Daniel do? _____

       Who reveals secrets? _____

Did Daniel take any credit for the secrets he had been given? _____

_____

Did God's secrets help Daniel to prosper? _____

f. 1 Corinthians 2:9-12

Have our eyes seen, our ears heard or our hearts known the things God has prepared for those who love Him? _____

According to verse 10, what does God reveal to us? _____

_____

How does He reveal these things? _____

According to verse 12, through the revelation we receive from the Spirit of God, what does God want us to know? _____

_____

This passage implies that there are some things we don't know, haven't seen and haven't heard. Yet God wants us to know the things He has freely given to us. It sounds like a contradiction: on one hand, we don't know them; but on the other hand, He wants us to know them. Thank God, we are able to know these wonderful things by revelation, through communion and fellowship with the Spirit of God!

g. Ephesians 1:15-19

What can we pray for according to verses 17-19? _____

_____

_____

Just one secret, one revelation, one creative idea from God can change your life!

2. Wisdom, invention, and creativity:

a. Proverbs 8:11,12

What is wisdom better than? _____

What does wisdom find out? _____

Through wisdom, God will give you creative ideas!

b. Exodus 26:1,31; 28:6; 28:15; 31:4; 35:33,35; 36:8,35; 38:23; 39:3,8; 1 Samuel 16:16,18; 1 Kings 7:14; 1 Chronicles 22:15; 25:7; 2 Chronicles 2:7,13,14; Daniel 1:4

In these verses, we see God assigning and equipping people with the ability to devise "cunning" works. List the various types of "cunning" works and abilities:

CUNNING: This is a word about creativity, innovation, and invention! We see these Hebrew words translated as the word "cunning."

"Chashab" (pronounced khaw-shab).[1] Its meaning includes to think, plan, weave, invent, fabricate, imagine, compute, devise and forecast.

"Machashabah" (pronounced makh-ash-aw-baw) or "machashebeth" (pronounced makh-ash-eh-beth).[2] Its meaning includes a contrivance, a machine, intention, plan, device, imagination, invented.

"Yada"(pronounced yaw-dah).[3] Its meaning includes to know, to ascertain by seeing, observation, recognition, comprehend, discern, discover, knowledge, perceive, privy to, skillful, and have understanding.

"Chakam" (pronounced khaw-kawm).[4] Its meaning includes wise, intelligent, skillful, and artful.

"Daath" (pronounced dah-ath).[5] Its meaning includes knowledge.

In other words, we see that God fills people with "wisdom of heart" to devise "cunning works" that includes God filling people with wisdom to think, plan, invent, imagine, fabricate, compute, forecast, contrive, devise, see, know, observe, recognize comprehend, discern, discover, perceive, be privy to His knowledge, be skillful, have understanding, be wise intelligent, artful, and to have knowledge.

Do you see creativity and innovation here? How exciting! As we seek God and His wisdom for His purposes He fills us with incredible creativity. He allows us to be privy to His knowledge and to recognize and to invent, to discover...the sky is the limit!

c. 2 Chronicles 26:11-15

God blessed King Uzziah. We see his "cunning" men inventing something in verse 15. Describe this creative invention: _____

What was the result of the success of this invention? _____
_____

Creativity and invention gave Uzziah great success and a great name. Unfortunately, we see that King Uzziah was lifted up in pride as a result, but as God blesses us through creativity and invention, we have the choice to stay humble and contrite in God's sight, giving Him the praise for our success.

D. ARE YOU FRAMING YOUR WORLD OF PROSPERITY WITH YOUR WORDS?

As we conclude this chapter, let's take a look at one very practical way we can begin to change our world — speaking God's Word. We can reach our greatest God-given potential. We can think big faith thoughts. We can be creative. Our minds have been renewed by God's Word. Now it's time to put God's Word in our mouths. By speaking God's Word, we can literally frame, or reframe, our world!

1. Proverbs 6:2

   What does this say our words can do to us? _____

   Perhaps in the past you have been ensnared by your own words. Words of defeat, doubt, failure, rejection, and the like, can literally trap and cause you to descend into a downward spiral. It does matter what you say! Let's look at Scriptures that will help you to escape any previous entrapments.

2. Proverbs 13:2,3

   What does the fruit of man's mouth produce? _____

   If we keep our mouth, what do we keep? _____

3. Proverbs 18:20,21

   What are we satisfied with? _____

   What is in the power of the tongue? _____

   If you love (and respect) the power of the words coming out your mouth, and speak accordingly, what will you have? _____
   _____

   In a sense, our words are like seeds that produce fruit. What type of fruit are you planting with the seeds of your mouth? _____

4. Matthew 12:33-37

   Jesus talked about the importance of our words and the importance of the type of fruit our mouth produces.

In verse 33, we are likened to a "tree." A tree is known by what? _____

_____

Our mouth produces the fruit that determines what kind of tree we have!

Our mouth speaks out of the abundance of what? _____

A good man "brings forth" good things. In the context of this passage, how does he bring them forth? _____

_____

In other words, we are naturally going to speak with our mouth the things that are in our heart in abundance. We are going to "bring forth" good (or bad) things with our mouth, from the treasure that is in our heart. If God's Word fills our heart in abundance, we will speak His Word, and His Word will "come forth" into our life. We will enjoy good fruit!

5. Mark 11:23

    After reading this passage, write down what Jesus said about the importance of what you say. _____

    _____

6. James 3:3-5

    To what three things is our tongue compared?

    _____

    _____

    _____

    What does the bit do in a horse's mouth? _____

    _____

    That little bit can turn a big horse around in the same way our little tongue can turn our whole life around!

    What does the helm (rudder) do on a ship? _____

    _____

    A little helm can steer a big ship from one port to another in the same way that our little tongue can steer our whole life from one port to another!

    What can a spark (little fire) do? _____

    _____

    A little spark can start a great forest fire in the same way our little tongue can start a great "faith fire" in our lives!

7. Hebrews 11:3

How was the world framed (prepared, made perfect)? _____

_____

Things that are seen were made of what? _____

_____

God framed the world with His Word. He made the world which we can see from things which did not appear by using His Word!

In the same way, perhaps there are some things in your life that are not appearing at this moment. For example, perhaps you aren't experiencing prosperity to the degree that you desire and the success which you know to be God's will. Let's say it doesn't appear to be evident in your life. You can change that by putting God's Word in your mouth! You can begin to frame your world with your words based upon God's Word. And God's plan for your success and prosperity will become evident in your life!

What you believe about yourself on the inside and what you say with your mouth is the world in which you live. Can you see areas where you need to change what you are saying — areas where your tongue can become the bit, helm, or spark, to effect the changes you desire? What can you say about yourself, your spouse, your children, your family and friends, your church, your co-workers and your neighbors that is in line with God's Word? You might want to consider using faith-filled sentences that begin with:

I can...
I will...
I know...
I believe...
I am...
I have...
I receive...

So, in concluding this chapter, are you convinced that God wants you to get a grip on prosperous living?

God has a wonderful plan for your life, and it is rich with potential! It's my sincere prayer that, as you have studied God's Word in this chapter, He will continue to give you His grace to reach your greatest God-given potential for His glory and for the advancement of His kingdom. In doing so, I am confident that you will progressively experience the prosperous life God has intended for you all along!

E. PERSONAL APPLICATION: WRITE THE VISION

In Habakkuk 2:2,3 we are told: **Write the vision, and make it plain upon tables, that he may run that readeth it. For the vision is yet for an appointed time, but at the end it shall speak, and not lie: though it tarry, wait for it; because it will surely come, it will not tarry.**

As you have studied through this workbook, I believe God has given you more of His vision for your life and prosperity. So it would be a helpful exercise to take some time to "write the vision" God has given you on paper. As you read it, you can run with God's vision for you. This chart may help you to determine where you are, where you want to be and how, with God's help, you plan to get there. Think about each of these categories as you write your vision down.

CATEGORIES	WHERE AM I NOW?	WHERE DO I WANT TO BE?	HOW WILL I GET THERE?
SPIRITUAL LIFE			
MENTALLY			
EMOTIONAL LIFE			
PHYSICAL BODY			
FINANCIALLY			
SOCIAL LIFE			
VOCATION			
MARRIAGE/FAMILY			
SERVICE			

CONCLUSION

I pray this workbook has been an encouragement and an inspiration to your faith. My desire is that God has expanded your vision for prosperous living and that you will begin to experience all He has for you — not just in theory, but in the reality of your daily experience. I hope I have conveyed in this workbook the passion I feel in my spirit about God's desire to prosper and to bless His people for eternal purposes. I trust the Holy Spirit will light a fire inside of you and give you God's grace and wisdom to walk in it to a greater measure!

We have covered a lot of ground in this workbook, so I recommend that you study through it again and again, reviewing what you have learned while continually building your faith and acting upon God's Word.

If this study has been meaningful to you, consider sharing it with others.

Our mission is, and continues to be:

> **...Christ in you, the hope of glory: whom we preach, warning every man, and teaching every man in all wisdom; that we may present every man perfect in Christ Jesus: whereunto I also labour, striving according to his working, which worketh in me mightily.**

> **Colossians 1:27-29**

END NOTES

Chapter One

[1]*Strong's Exhaustive Concordance*: A Concise Dictionary of the Words in the Hebrew Bible; with their renderings in the Authorized English Version, James Strong, S.T.D., LLD, 1890, Baker Book House, Grand Rapids, Michigan, pg. 116, #7965.

[2]Strong's p. 92, entry# 6238.

[3]Strong's p. 50, entry# 3276.

[4]*Thayer Greek-English Lexicon of the New Testament Numerically coded to Strong's Exhaustive Concordance*, 1977 by Baker Book House Company, author Joseph Henry Thayer, D.D., Mott Media, Milford, Michigan, p. 273, #2222.

[5]*Thayer Greek-English Lexicon of the New Testament Numerically coded to Strong's Exhaustive Concordance*, 1977 by Baker Book House Company, author Joseph Henry Thayer, D.D., Mott Media, Milford, Michigan pg. 505-506, #4053.

[6]Strong's, p. 33, entry #2137.

Thayer Lexicon, p. 260-261, entry #2137.

[7]For further study on God's plan for the prosperity of your physical body, we suggest you obtain the workbook, *Getting a Grip on the Basics of Health and Healing*.

[8]Strong's, p. 121, entry# 8317.

[9]Strong's, p. 106, entry# 7230.

[10]Strong's, p. 106, entry# 7235.

[11]Strong's, p. 57, entry# 4053.

[12]*Thompson Chain-Reference Bible*, Tables in *The Thompson Comprehensive Bible Helps*, (Indianapolis, Indiana: B. B. Kirkbride, 1964), p. 142, #3531, and #3536.

Dakes, Complete Concordance-Cyclopedic Index "Money" column 2.

Smith's Bible Dictionary, by William Smith, L.L.D., Thomas Nelson Publishers, Nashville, Camden, New York, Sixteenth printing May 1981, p 739.

"Weights and Measures" p. 813, "Jewish Weights, Measures, Time and Money."

Economist Desk Companion, How to Measure, Convert, Calculate and Define Practically Anything, United States of America Weights and Measures, 1992, Economist Publisher, London England, p. 20.

[13]Strong's, p. 50, entry #3254.

[14]Strong's, p. 122, entry# 8393.

[15]Strong's, p. 106, entry# 7235.

[16]Strong's, p. 96, entry# 6509.

[17]Strong's, p. 106, entry# 7235.

[18]Strong's, p. 108, entry# 7399.

[19]Strong's, p. 52, entry# 3426.

[20]Strong's, p. 32, entry# 1952.

[21]Strong's, p. 9, entry# 214.

Chapter Two

[1]Strong's, p. 55, entry# 3627.

Chapter Four

[1]Strong's, p. 17, entry# 842.

[2]Strong's, p. 16, entry# 715.

[3]Strong's, p.8, entry# 146.

[4]Strong's, p. 23, entry# 1214.

[5]Thayer Greek-English Lexicon, p. 516, #4124.

[6]Strong's, p. 23, entry# 1215.

Chapter Five

[1]For further study along the lines of God's will concerning sickness and health, we suggest our book, *Getting a Grip on the Basics of Health and Healing.*

[2]Strong's, p. 70, entry# 4643.

[3]Strong's, p. 26, entry# 1431.

[4]Average gold price, Wall Street Journal, January 1997.

[5]*Thompson Chain-Reference Bible,* Tables in *The Thompson Comprehensive Bible Helps,* (Indianapolis, Indiana: B. B. Kirkbride, 1964), p. 142, #3531, and #3536.

Dakes, *Complete Concordance-Cyclopedic Index* "Money" column 2.

Smith's Bible Dictionary, by William Smith, L.L.D., Thomas Nelson Publishers, Nashville, Camden, New York, Sixteenth printing May 1981, p. 739.

"Weights and Measures" p. 813 "Jewish Weights, Measures, Time and Money."

Economist Desk Companion, How to Measure, Convert, Calculate and Define Practically Anything, United States of America Weights and Measures, 1992, Economist Publisher, London England, p. 20.

Chapter Six

[1]Finis Jennings Dake. (*Dake's Annotated Reference Bible.*), New Testament, p. 109, reference "o", Column 1 (Lawrenceville, Georgia: Dake Bible Sales, 1963).

[2]Dake, p. 118, reference "f", column 1.

Strong's, p. 77, entry# 5509.

The Complete Biblical Library, Greek English Dictionary, SIGMA-OMEGA, 1986, Thoralf Gilbrant and Tor Inge Gilbrant, Published by The Complete Biblical Library, Springfield MO, p. 503-504.

[3]William Smith, L.L.D., *Smith's Bible Dictionary.* (Nashville, Tennessee: Thomas Nelson), p. 497.

Chapter Seven

[1]Strong's, p. 70, entry# 4643.

[2]Strong's, p. 27, entry# 1654.

Chapter Eight

[1]Strong's, p. 39, entry# 2451, 2452, 2454.

[2]Strong's, p. 20, entry# 998.

[3]Strong's, p. 58, entry# 3820.

[4]Strong's, p. 92, entry# 6195.

[5]Strong's, p.116, entry# 7919.

[6]Strong's, p. 116, entry# 7922.

[7]Strong's, p. 123, entry# 8454.

[8]Strong's, p. 84, entry# 5647.

[9]Strong's, p. 118, entry# 8104.

Chapter Nine

[1]Strong's, p. 44, entry# 2803.

[2]Strong's p. 65, entry# 4284.

[3]Strong's p. 47, entry# 3045.

[4]Strong's p. 39, entry# 2450.

[5]Strong's p. 31, entry# 1847.

Beth Jones is a Bible teacher and author, a wife and the mother of four children who ministers the Word in a relevant and inspiring way by sharing down-to-earth insights. Beth is author of the 5 books in the "Getting A Grip On The Basics" series, a popular Bible study program. She also wrote "Baby Boomer Trivia" published by Honor Books, Tulsa, OK. She received her BA in Communications from Boston University, Boston, Massachusetts and her post-graduate Bible training and ordination through Rhema Bible Training Center in Tulsa, Oklahoma. She and her husband Jeff serve as the Senior Pastors of Kalamazoo Valley Family Church, a growing congregation of genuine believers in Portage, Michigan.

The Complete "Get A Grip" Series Includes:

Getting a Grip on the Basics
Getting a Grip on the Basics of Health and Healing
Getting a Grip on the Basics of Prosperous Living
Getting a Grip on the Basics of Serving God
Getting a Grip on the Basics For Kids

Available from Valley Press Publishers or your local bookstore.

VALLEY PRESS
PUBLISHERS

Portage, MI 49024

The Vision of Valley Press Publishers

"We are committed to developing a global publishing company where books, tapes, videos, CDs and various resource materials are produced to help leaders, believers and seekers live by great faith, live out the great commandment and live for the great commission."